CJ:
I'm really _____
_____ on your show on August 11Th

GIVE

A

DAMN!®

The Ticket to Cultural Change

Individually, you make a difference,

Collectively we change the world!

thanks so much for your support!

Mark S. Lewis

#1 Best Selling Author

Mark S. Lewis

3/15/21

Dedicated to my mom,

Shirley B. Lewis
(April 9, 1926 – November 19, 2012)

She had a wonderful and loving heart!

Mom truly knew how to

GIVE A DAMN!

About the Author

Mark S. Lewis has a very diverse background, working for big business (IBM for 13 years), starting and selling successful businesses, and helping entities with successful turnaround strategies. As a business mentor, coach and consultant, Mark has facilitated and moderated CEO Round tables for the past several years, helping hundreds of CEOs and individuals accelerate their growth, both personally and professionally. His philosophy is based on creating the business strategies that engage a positive cultural environment across all functional operations that everyone wants to be part of. It all begins with a give a damn attitude.

If you want to create a cultural environment that improves the productivity of your employees, and leads to remarkable success and happiness, have Mark engage your team with his give a damn philosophy and you will never look back. His presentations provide powerful motivation for success in both your personal and business life.

4

How a Culture Change Can
Lead to Explosive Growth and Happiness

Want to personally grow as an individual? Want to have a happier life? Want to change how your employees think about your organization to help make it grow? Want to improve customer service? Want your employees to achieve greater success? Want to make a positive difference in your life and the lives of others?

If you answered yes to any of these questions, Mark is available to provide a 30 – 45 minute presentation to individuals or your group on motivating, engaging and implementing the Give a Damn cultural philosophy for growth, success and happiness. Please reach out for availability.

All inquiries, including bulk purchases of the Give A Damn book philosophy for success, including discounts, should be addressed to:

Mark S. Lewis
MSL Properties LLC
6709 Avenue A
New Orleans, LA 70124
www.giveadamnbook.com
mlewis@giveadamnbook.com
(504) 905-4646

HERE'S TO YOUR SUCCESS!!

Mission Statement: To make every person and organization happier by changing and enhancing their mindset in a more positive and serving direction towards others. This results in making the world a better place to live. This is accomplished by educating and promoting the values and principles of the Give A Damn philosophy so that every person and organization implements them daily.

5

Foreword

When I think about individuals who embody a Give a Damn attitude, Steve Gleason certainly comes to mind, and is at the top of my list. Steve Gleason played for the New Orleans Saints NFL football team from 2000 – 2008. He will always be remembered for the punt he blocked against the Atlanta Falcons the night that the Superdome reopened for the first time after Hurricane Katrina. In fact, he became a symbol of the city's resilience after such a terrible storm. A few years later, Steve was diagnosed with Amyotrophic Lateral Sclerosis (ALS), a terminal neuromuscular disease, otherwise known as Lou Gehrig's disease. Steve has lost so much in terms of physical strength and ability, but his intellect and positive attitude keep him going and make him an inspiration to so many. The blocked punt was significant, but what he is doing for others in the fight against Lou Gehrig's disease is what makes Steve so special.

Often, in the face of such a frightening diagnosis, the only thing that is most important to Steve is his family, and not what he would call a focus on my "self." He turns inward and focuses on his family rather than being consumed by the daily struggles that come with a serious medical condition. Steve, however, is determined to help find a cure for ALS and also to inspire others by continuing to live his life to the fullest, despite his diagnosis. He has helped to provide countless others suffering from neuromuscular diseases or injuries with cutting edge technology, equipment and services. He partnered with Microsoft to develop a program which allows people to do many things with their eyes, such as drive a wheelchair, control appliances, lights in the house, and much more. As Steve would say, he is not imprisoned by his wheelchair, he is liberated by it. In fact, he will tell you that technology saved his life, and his initiative with technology alone has given others with Lou Gehrig's disease a new purpose and lease on life. He and his friends and family started "Team Gleason" to generate public awareness for ALS, and they continue to raise funds to empower those with Lou Gehrig's disease to live a rewarding life, and ultimately to find a cure. In fact, 20% of all proceeds from the sale of this book go to Team Gleason

Steve has been involved in countless initiatives to find a cure and his passion and drive is making great progress. He is the ultimate Give a Damn role model who is using his personal diagnosis and challenges to motivate and inspire others. He sees his situation as an opportunity to inform and inspire people from all walks of life. I recently had the chance to ask Steve some questions about his life experiences and what keeps him going toward helping others. He typed his responses to the questions below, by using the motion of his eyes. As Steve said, "I type with my eyes. So if what I say in my answers sounds crazy, they probably are." And I would say to that: "Those who are crazy enough to change the world, are usually the ones who do."

Question 1: Given the many principles expressed in this book, how have they had an influence not only on your upbringing, your professional football career but also the battle with your medical condition? How have you changed or transitioned as a person over the years?

Steve: Growing up, I think the principle that most influenced me was the concept that, the best way to help yourself is to first serve and help others. I do not think this is as being "totally selfless," instead I call it "self interest." The concept was instilled in me by my parents and the high school I went to – Gonzaga Prep. Despite my ALS diagnosis and the challenges I have had to face, I knew I wanted to continue to live a productive life, so I set out to help others do that same thing with their lives.

Question 2: How have your (what I would refer to as Give A Damn) principles had an influence on the inspiration and public management of your illness?

Steve: With the public management of my diagnosis, it is not about me. It's more about OUR public management because with ALS, and like most other illnesses, it affects the entire family.

7

With our family's management of ALS constantly in the public lens, I believe the most important principle that we followed was being open, honest, and forthcoming about our struggles, our pain, and our vulnerabilities.

Everyone experiences suffering at some point in their life. It's the most real part of our human existence. We could potentially replace, "I think therefore I am," with "I suffer therefore I am." Despite this common thread that links us in our existence, we rarely share our weakness with each other. Our family's choice was to share our struggles, as well as our triumphs publicly because I believe it will help other people see themselves in us in some way.

Question 3: How have these principles had an influence on the Team Gleason foundation and your philanthropic goals and how has it made you feel?

Steve: With all the love and support that I have received from family and friends, despite my ALS diagnosis, I have been able to find a way to lead a productive and purposeful life by helping others as best I can. Despite so many challenges, I feel like I've been able to conquer ALS. Our foundation (Team Gleason) and the resulting philanthropic venture (Answer ALS), allows us to help others live triumphant and meaningful lives – to be fellow conquerors; instead of being forced to fade away and die a silent death. Together we (as you would say – Give A Damn) are empowering families to overcome the injustice of ALS. Most importantly, we're taking positive steps toward our ultimate goal – Ending ALS.

Question 4: After everything that you have been through, what keeps you going?

Steve: Despite the abundant struggles that many people face in life, I've been able to find meaning and a purpose in life. I believe that all humans seek to live a productive, purposeful life, yet few truly find this. Purpose and meaning keep me going. I have no intention to "hang in there" or "survive." I intend to keep living a purposeful, productive life, and do what I love.

NO WHITE FLAGS!

Steve Gleason

PS Thanks Mark. Nice work.

Introduction

For all the people who read my first edition of *Give a Damn*, I thank you. In the first version, I felt there was something missing. I needed more examples that might engage readers and inspire a Give a Damn philosophy in people and businesses all over the world. I received so many great comments on how to take *Give a Damn* to the next level that I needed to create this second edition. So, I did.

My dream with Give a Damn is for this philosophy to be adopted by the entire world. Who says it can't be done? They say that people who are crazy enough to change the world are the only ones who do. There are so many great examples: Steve Jobs, Nelson Mandela, Martin Luther King Jr., Albert Einstein, Steve Gleason, and the list goes on and on. I would love to be one of these people. Not one of them did it alone, however. Given the direction our society is headed today—and it's not pretty—I want to make our world a better place for both present and future generations. And I need your help.

The goal of Give a Damn is to help people develop a greater awareness of the thoughts and actions that currently and/or eventually lead people to selfish and irresponsible behaviors. It cuts across all industries, all organizations, all nationalities—everyone. My goal is for this book to guide you and others toward a better mindset. We *can* make a difference, one person at a time.

When I talk to people about my philosophy and the concepts needed by society to implement change, most everyone agrees. Few would argue against values such as accountability, responsibility, trustworthiness, caring for others, character, and generosity of spirit. However, while most would agree with these values, most peoples' actions suggest otherwise. Actions always speak louder than words, and it's not happening.

I am blessed to have Steve Gleason support our Give a Damn initiative with his foreword. Steve is the true hero here. Just imagine if you had to endure what he has gone through in life; yet, at the same time, he is driven to help others. His purpose in life is to ensure that others do not suffer the same fate as he has, so he fights like a dog, overcoming every obstacle imaginable to find a cure for Lou Gehrig's disease. It takes a very special person to do this. Steve truly cares about others and he has the respect and admiration of everyone he meets. And people care deeply about him as well. You just wonder in amazement how he does it.

With the help of Molly Kramer and her team at Model Content, the revision of this edition was focused on enhancing readers' engagement in Give a Damn principles, with clear justification of why this is so important. After several years, even I can state that I don't always embody the Give a Damn philosophy. Because of the tremendous noise and societal challenges that we have to face every day, it's very difficult. Yet, I know that what I have learned over the past several years and what I have done to implement Give A Damn principles has helped improve many lives, including my own. I am happy about this.

I am not perfect, but it is better to strive for perfection and miss than to strive for imperfection and hit it.

With this second edition, I want the same for you. When you read this book, I hope you will understand and embrace the many themes and initiatives that I present: to act in big and small ways to help others, to be happier and more successful, to fulfill your purpose in life, and to make Give a Damn a big part of what you do no matter what path you take. Together we can push society back in the right direction, one person at a time, until, collectively, *we* can make a difference. Give a Damn is the ticket to cultural change.

I hope you will join our Give a Damn movement at www.giveadamnbook.com. Thank you for your support in making a difference.

Contents

Chapter 1 – Why I'm Fed Up and You Should Be Too!

In the spring of 2009, the call came in. The mayor of New Orleans needed an independent information technology firm. This was the opportunity I'd been hoping for in my years of advocacy for local tech businesses. But it came during a troubled time for the Nagin administration.

There had been some bad press surrounding the deletion of data on Mayor C. Ray Nagin's computer. It was the beginning of the end for the man who had come into office with a reputation for being above the fray. In the 2002 mayoral race, Nagin emerged as a reformer. A business leader with no political experience, he pledged to clean up corruption. A taxi bureau crackdown in the early months of his administration gave us confidence that he would walk the walk.

In August 2005, Hurricane Katrina landed on our shores. It brought wind, storm surge, and flooding. There was so much destruction and death. The storm also planted the seed of Nagin's undoing.

Four years later, our city was still reeling. Amid our grief, a local news reporter had to resort to a public records lawsuit against the reform-minded mayor. In failing to meet the public records request for email and calendar items from Nagin and his communications director, his administration was found to be in "flagrant violation" of the law. The judge assigned the highest penalties allowed.

At the time, Nagin stated that he needed to delete information because his computer needed more space. However, there was no mention of him ever backing up the computer. As a result, the judge ordered the city to hire a firm to recover the data. Several firms, including the non-profit Louisiana Technology Council (LTC), which I led, were asked to submit a bid on the project. The target was the missing calendar items and emails from the prior year.

Under normal circumstances, I would never bid on these opportunities directly. As they came in, I would relay them to at least three LTC member companies, and they would submit their own proposals. However, my thinking on this was different.

From the day I first took over the LTC, a primary goal was to engage the city of New Orleans to do business with locals, rather than continuing to outsource most tech contracts to non-Louisiana companies. I had assumed the association presidency around the time Nagin was elected mayor, and our multiple overtures to the administration had gotten us nowhere. Despite the LTC's advocacy, our local tech companies continued to face rejection at their own city hall.

At long last, I saw this data recovery project as the tech community's big chance. I wanted to prove that our member companies were just as good as anyone in the country. So, I immediately began to build a project team. I contacted two LTC member firms with expertise in data recovery.

I received a quote from the member firms for $15,000 but asked if they could do it for half the price. I also told them that, based on the city's history of slow payment for work performed, payment would be either really late or never happen at all. My member companies understood this, and we provided a quote to the city for $8,500 to do the work.

Underbidding paid off. The LTC won the bid and was issued a purchase order to get started. Our big chance now was under way, and I was ecstatic.

On Friday, May 8, 2009, the LTC and the Nagin administration had our first face-to-face meeting to kick off the contract. We told the city the precise processes we would implement in our attempt to recover the data from the server, going all the way back to 2005.

That day, seven of us sat at the table—three from the city and four members representing the LTC. We discussed the general structure of the city's network and mail servers, and we agreed that work could begin immediately. The city had two mail servers. At the end of the meeting, copies of the Microsoft Exchange databases from both servers were being ported over to the city's main server. That's where our team would start the initial work to recover the data.

We scheduled our next appointment with the city for the following Wednesday, and my project partners began to implement their work.

Then all hell broke loose. But I'll get into that later.

People who don't give a damn are everywhere. At first, I thought this complete lack of regard for others was just in my city. But it's not just in certain geographical areas. It's not a city attitude at all. It's prevalent across the world. This gets down to the very core of our society. But what is that core? Do people really understand what it is?

I'm discouraged by the acts of selfishness, irresponsibility, complacency, and even violence that we all observe in our daily news headlines. Our standards of acceptability permit, and even promote, behavior that is way too self-centered.

Common sense and basic reasoning are two traits that appear to be lacking in a lot of people these days. In their place, you'll find a toxic mindset. Too many people just think about the job they have to do or how things might affect them personally. Society's core has simply shifted to a self-centered attitude, thereby resulting in individuals ignoring other people. And it hurts everyone.

In my opinion, there are three reasons most people don't actively give a damn:

1. They really just don't care;

2. They don't know how self-serving their actions are; or, more importantly,

3. They know they have a problem, but don't know how to change or fix it.

Those people that fall into the first group do not believe in the importance of serving others because they are focused on serving themselves. Nothing else really matters to them. They go about their business or lives and only worry about their own problems. They don't care about others. They fail to realize how important giving a damn really is, in their own life and for society as a whole.

People in the second group are simply unaware of their own attitudes, their actions (or lack thereof), and the effects of their behavior on others. They might mean well, but they don't realize how self-serving their actions really are, and I am not sure it's entirely their fault. They just don't understand.

People in the third group mean well, but fail to change their actual behavior, unless doing so will benefit them in some way. Although they set out to make change, they are constantly bumping up against both the internal and external powerful forces of self-interest, which all have a profound effect on their own deeply ingrained habits.

I don't know which category Nagin fell into. Maybe he did, at one point, believe in his promised work of reform. Maybe he really thought he would be able to stand above the corruption that Louisiana has so long been known for. But by the time he was under investigation, he might have felt there was no way out and could only continue down the path of deception he'd already paved.

After the LTC's kick-off meeting with the city, we began the work as discussed. The LTC group included Christopher Reade at Carrollton Technology Partners and Wayne Latour at CommTech Industries. We began reviewing several copies of data from a variety of Microsoft Exchange databases culled from several sources, including backup tapes and offline storage devices.

Shortly after my LTC project partners began their work at the city office, I received a call from one of them. I was told that, about an hour after we wrapped up a pre-kickoff conference call with the city on May 5, someone used software to deliberately delete two of the 61 mailboxes belonging to the administration.

The two deleted mailboxes belonged to Nagin and the city's chief information officer. The other 59 mailboxes were left intact. Now what?

I asked my project partners if they could recover the data that was deleted. The answer was yes, but they could not be certain what the data might look like. Since this had gotten much deeper, I then looked for an expert company in digital forensics. I found one locally in Digital Forensics Solutions and our project partner there, Golden Richard. We continued to do everything we could to recover the data, but planned to withhold our findings from the city until after getting all the data onto a hard drive.

We actually had no choice. If we were to go back to the city and tell them that a violation of the law had been committed prior to us recovering the data, what do you think might have happened? Do you think additional improprieties might have occurred? Obviously, we could not take that chance.

We did, however, notify the FBI of our findings, and we formulated a plan that would allow us to go public with our general findings without violating the non-disclosure agreement that protected the data itself. My thinking was this: If you knowingly withhold information that is against the law, you are committing a violation yourself, and I did not want the LTC or our member companies to be complicit.

There were two servers that we needed to recover the data from. One was an older server that was replaced in 2008. This was the one that was missing the two mailboxes, including the mayor's, and we focused on this server first. The second server would come later, but wouldn't be nearly as important.

To our surprise, the city allowed us to remotely recover the data and we had access to this server on a 24-hour basis. Finally, we got all the data—although the state of the data was a complete mess. Imagine going up 10,000 feet in an airplane with one million sheets of paper, throwing them all out the window, and then trying to put those sheets back together in numerical order. That is what the data looked like. However, our forensics company was able to write a program to put the data together. But when they began to

18

run the program, the LTC was suddenly fired from our city contract. Our work grounded to a halt.

More on this later. Just suffice it to say that I could write a book on this one event alone.

The bottom line was that we were able to recover Nagin's calendar and email items going back several years, with the majority of the roughly 1,600 appointments being from 2007 through the first half of 2009. We also recovered notes, contacts, and other elements of the deleted mailbox. However, the rnagin@mnomail.com messages from before February 2009 remained elusive.

Way too many people fail to understand the value of really giving a damn about others. The big question in their minds is, "If I don't look after myself first, who will?"

If I told people to give a damn and by doing so they could make 15 times their annual earnings, do you think they would? If I told people that, by starting to give a damn today they'd be absolved of their past misdeeds, do you think they would? Absolutely! The problem with this type of thinking is that they would do it only for the money or the get-out-of-jail-free card, meaning that they are still thinking about themselves. It is still a self-centered attitude. And the value of giving a damn doesn't stem from material rewards.

Giving a damn is not a superficial change. Starting on the outside by changing behavior is a good start, but it won't lead to a lasting change in our society. We have to change our thought patterns. It is not about what society can do for you, it's about what you can do for society and your fellow human beings. How much clearer can this get? The more you do for society, the more you will get in return.

Just think of others, act accordingly, and you will reap the benefits—though those benefits won't always be material. The emotional benefit can be just as rewarding. In other words, you should give a damn because it is the right thing to do, and it is what our world really needs.

For every action you take, there is going to be a reaction or response of some kind. The truth always wins. What you do wrong (lie, steal, cheat, etc.) will always come out sooner or later. Always.

I don't mean that a lie will always be uncovered, or that a criminal will always be prosecuted. And yes, there will be times when you derive no obvious benefit from your good actions. However, when all is said and done, both society and your ultimate maker will reward you. It's just the right thing to do!

People who give a damn react to others in a positive but also giving way. Yet, they don't think they will get something out of what they give. Ironically, giving and reacting in a positive way will naturally lead to something that will benefit you, without you even expecting it. It will always come back to you in some way.

The Give a Damn philosophy can be translated into caring about what other people want and need more than what you want and need. Of course, you cannot help people all of the time, and there will be people who will try to take advantage of you. But putting the needs of others above your own is always a good motto to live by.

Give a Damn people aren't perfect. Sometimes we forget or slip up. Sometimes we act in selfish ways. Occasionally we flake out on commitments, break the rules, and act with disrespect or even cruelty. But when it happens, we don't blame others or outside circumstances. And more times than not, Give a Damn people will be rewarded because they apologize, admit their mistake, take responsibility for it, and then fix it. Sometimes the consequences can be difficult to accept, but the Give a Damn person does it anyway.

The reward doesn't always come in the form of another's forgiveness. We may still have to pay a fine or suffer some other penalty for our mistake. The reward for taking responsibility may only be a spiritual or emotional one. These rewards do occur, however. That's because I firmly believe that altruism—selfless concern for the well-being of others—is in our fundamental nature as humans.

20

Nagin may have forgotten this. Or he may have never known.

My next example really hurts.

At 78 years old, Angel Arce Torres was retired from the forklift job he had held for 30 years in West Hartford, Conn. He was enjoying his time as a grandfather and great-grandfather, as well as a volunteer at the local housing authority's youth division.

Several years ago, Torres had purchased some milk on Park Street in Hartford, an area notorious for its high crime rate. Not far away, Luis Negron was chasing another motorist in a dispute over money. As Torres walked back across the street from the store, he was suddenly struck by Negron's car.

The vehicle was only traveling about 20 miles per hour, but the impact was significant, causing Torres to flip over and land on his head in the middle of the street. Negron did not stop and, as Torres lay there injured, no one came to help. Police said that four people called 911, but no one acted to help the man directly or even divert traffic as he lay on the concrete surface. Car after car swerved around him and went on their way.

The horrifying wait for help went on for a minute and a half, as captured by a surveillance camera. I watched the video myself and it felt like hours. There had to be at least 20 people who were aware of the incident, and not one of them bothered to help. You cannot imagine how many cars went past him without stopping. Stop and look at your watch and see how long a minute and a half can be!

Now, if you were driving your car past this man and noticed it was your grandfather, what would you do? Would you come to his aid immediately? Damn right you would. The fact that no one helped for over a minute was mind-boggling to me.

Maybe people were scared by what they saw or feared getting involved because they might be blamed if something went wrong. Excuses that were communicated by residents in the high-crime area included fear of being labeled a snitch—and suffering the consequences. Randy Cohen, then an ethics columnist for the

New York Times, saw herd mentality at work in the crowd's cruel indifference. But any excuse not to help this man is a lousy one. This is a classic example of people who just did not give a damn.

As a result of the hit-and-run, and possibly the long wait for help as well, Torres was paralyzed from the waist down. He needed a ventilator to breathe, and then suffered kidney failure and other medical issues. After a year, he'd lost any awareness that his loved ones were keeping vigil. He was removed from life support.

Torres' tragedy leaves me wondering what even makes us human—especially when I see how animals can act in a similar situation.

In another video I've seen, a dog is the victim of a hit-and-run. After getting hit by a car, the dog was lying in the middle of a major highway, yet was still alive. As the video played, not one person stopped to help remove the dog from further harm. But another dog did. It dodged oncoming traffic to come to the rescue. The second dog ran over to the victim, grabbed him with his mouth, and carried him out of harm's way, nearly getting hit several times. And guess what? The victim lived.

What a contrast, huh? Human versus dog and the dog wins. In using these two examples, I don't mean to compare the value of the life of a human to the life of a dog. Torres was by all accounts a great man, and his family will be forever affected by the indignity and pain he suffered during his final year.

Rather, it's the behavior of the bystanders that I mean to compare. The dog saved one of its own kind because it knew how to give a damn. Is that possible? Dogs aren't supposed to have brains like we do but we could learn a thing or two from them. Aren't they always happy to see you? Don't they always want to please you?

Maybe the dog instinctively knew it was doing the right thing, no matter the personal risk involved in saving another. We humans are supposedly smarter than dogs. Maybe we need to incorporate this same kind of doggie attitude into our own behavior. Maybe we should have this kind of mentality: "Let me be the person my dog thinks I am."

So now you know why I am fed up. I see instances every day in which people just don't give a damn, and they can always find some form of justification or excuse for not doing so. I have simply had enough of the continuous inconsiderate attitudes and actions like those I've detailed so far.

Each of these cases—and even more minor occurrences like a poor attitude, disrespect, disregard, and negativity—forms another unstable building block in the self-serving structure of our society. I am fed up with people being too busy, greedy, and selfish to do the right thing or take responsibility for their actions. There seem to be no more consequences for our deeds, just excuses and bailouts. It always seems to be someone else's fault.

So, maybe people are too concerned about protecting their turf. I am not referring to physical turf like property or what you possess—though, obviously, both Nagin's corruption and Torres' death stemmed from a chase for wealth.

Here, turf refers to your non-physical personal interests. It is the domain you have in your mind, which keeps you focused on obtaining the best of material things. It's ego-driven. People who do not give a damn will step on anyone that gets in the way of this pursuit of the self-centered domain.

What people don't realize is that most others can help you rather than hurt you. If you are constantly protecting your turf and not doing things for people, over time you will lose friends, trust, others wanting to help you, confidence in yourself, your smile, and all the other truly good things in life. It perpetuates itself and gets worse over time. That's when you start feeling both the mental and physical pain.

Torres and his family suffered an unimaginable pain. But I imagine that the tragedy affected his community as well, sending waves of bewilderment and shame throughout—and forcing everyone to reconcile with the knowledge that they couldn't even rely on their own neighbors for the most basic assistance.

Everyone who reads this story throughout the world must question whether they are alone at their darkest moments. I know I did. And it hurts.

Nagin's corruption was a huge blow to the community. A punch in the gut during a time when New Orleans was still trying to find its footing amid all the physical devastation and personal loss that resulted from Hurricane Katrina.

Nagin's actions, however, are just one example of a broader problem. Society's self-serving attitude cannot lead to anything good in the future, and it certainly hasn't in the past. This cancerous pattern needs to be broken, and a Give a Damn attitude will cure it.

But no matter how fed up I am with the state of society and the actions of individuals, I still firmly believe in the positive nature of humanity. I think humans can do better. In fact, I think it's in our nature to do better. We just need to understand why it is so important.

Have you ever wondered about your purpose in life? Why were you born? Why do you exist? Why did God put you on this earth? Or, if you don't believe in God, why are you here? Can you honestly answer even one of these questions? I have asked hundreds of people these very same questions, and most do not have an answer.

Each one of us is destined to follow a different path. But surely our purpose is related to helping others in some way, isn't it? We were born to give a damn. We all have an inner voice guiding us toward these principles; there's just a tremendous amount of environmental effects, distractions, and outside noise that we have to filter out in order to hear it. We have to listen.

We must listen as closely as if it were always our own grandfather lying in the street, our own small business at risk of complicity with unlawful city hall activity, or our own turf facing violation. We must act as if we were just loving animals following a positive instinct. But we can't do it alone.

I don't think anyone would disagree that giving a damn is inherently good for individuals. It's aligned with our spirit, and it rewards us internally to live our lives with courtesy, altruism, commitment, and moral courage. And these values are also good for us as a herd. Collectively, a herd makes a big difference.

Remember that herd mentality that led Torres to lie alone in the street after his hit-and-run? That paralyzing force that kept bystanders from taking the basic compassionate step of redirecting traffic or holding the injured man's hand? That herd mentality can be harnessed for good. Give a Damn values, followed as a group, are contagious. They spread, creating a community of likeminded people.

And it is on this community level, this herd level, where the benefits multiply. Being a member of a Give a Damn community gives all of its members the ability to succeed in material and emotional ways. This new herd mentality can then reinforce positive behavior. Seeing it all around us makes it easier to live out the values consistently.

And a group can do so much more than one person can. Together, a tribe of like-minded folks can develop a self-sustaining growth of positive change, modeling the hopeful possibility to people who haven't joined the movement.

Give a Damn matters. It is the only mental state that can make this world better. I firmly believe this and my hope is that you also agree.

That is why the Give a Damn motto is:

Individually you make a difference,

Collectively we change the world!

Chapter 2 – How Did We Get Here?

What has happened to our society over the past few decades? It seems to me that we used to care more about others. In the first decade of the 21st century, researchers began to observe signs that young people might have less empathy than in previous generations.

Scholars have disagreed over the years on the best way to measure—or even define—empathy. Is it an intellectual activity or an emotional one? When we empathize with someone, are we taking on that person's exact emotions, or are we just having sympathy for their emotional state? Or maybe, scholars speculated, we empathize to reduce our own stress about what other people are going through.

Regardless of how you define it, there were signs that the younger generation was heading in the wrong direction. So, a research team at the University of Michigan's Research Center for Group Dynamics decided to tackle this issue head on. The team, led by social psychologist Sara H. Konrath, looked at all the studies to be found on American college students using a specific personality tool. Altogether, the studies included more than 13,000 students.

Their analysis, published in 2010, found that, from 1979 to 2009, there was a significant decline in perspective taking—in other words, considering things from another person's perspective—and empathic concern. These are the most central components of empathy, and the loss of these traits was particularly sharp in the last decade covered by the review.

The researchers speculated about why this trend was occurring. They pointed to a parallel rise in narcissism, meaning excessive or exotic interest in oneself and in one's physical appearance. Narcissism is linked in a negative way with empathy. It's hard to maintain an excessive interest in your own domain when you're not able to share the perspective of other members of your herd.

The researchers also saw some signs that violent acts, violent media, binge drinking, and bullying were on the rise. And they took note of societal changes in parenting and families.

In short, there are too many things going on in the world that breed a don't Give a Damn attitude. Most interesting to me, though, were the researchers' observations of media and technology.

"Media consumption appears to be increasingly popular as technological developments continue to advance," the analysis said. "Most obvious is the explosion of 'social' media." The Konrath team's review noted that today's teens aren't just using their phones for talking. Nearly all use smartphones for playing games, listening to music, and interacting on social media. More Americans than ever are using television and the internet at the same time.

These personal technology trends, the researchers said, may be affecting empathy by damaging our real-world relationships and our attention spans. And they are influencing us to prioritize self-expression over the welfare of others.

The researchers further theorized that, during the last decade covered by the review, reality TV may have been partly responsible for the findings. In the early 2000s, reality TV was rapidly gaining popularity and reality TV characters—the "less than empathic role models" that they are, as the review noted—grew into pop culture stars.

"Reality programming exploded with 'Survivor,' starting in 2000, and 'American Idol,' starting in 2002. Both shows revolve around single winners, multiple losers, aggressive characters, and rugged competition," the Konrath analysis said. Basically, in my eyes, these shows broadcast a self-centered attitude. Similarly, reality programming often depicts characters with "unfettered narcissism," according to the researchers.

So, based on the inability of these two traits to co-exist, the decline in empathy has been accompanied by a sharp rise in narcissism and self-oriented goals. In other words, before the significant rise of mobile devices, reality TV, and social media, our world used to embrace conscientious thinking a lot more than we do today.

I don't mean to imply that the world was perfect before 2000. There has always been bad behavior, and there have always been selfless people. But good deeds and a strong work ethic were much more highly valued before this quick change in media and technology. Cheating, lying, laziness, bad language, and greed were more likely to be frowned upon before, whereas now these behaviors are more likely to be tolerated, even among our leaders. Many individuals get away with them because they have no fear of repercussions if they are caught. In fact, these traits are almost admired!

Our society has deteriorated over the past several years because of our self-serving attitude. Society has transitioned into a me-centered culture. And I'm not just basing this off my own intuition; there are scientific studies to back it up! In 2006, the Pew Research Center reported that 64 percent of 18-years-olds surveyed said that making money was the most important goal of all!

These studies highlight two trends—a decline in empathy and a rise in narcissism—which affect us all. We have become a greedy culture. These qualities not only breed laziness, negativity, and disrespect, but also cruelty, crime, and violence. Who doesn't think that we have become a more selfish and violent society? I certainly do.

Over the past 20 years, we have progressively cared less for others than we used to, especially for people we don't know. Why is it that society generally does not give a damn? There are three primary reasons:

1. There is no foundation for how to give a damn. There is not nearly enough attention or focus on it in our schools or at home. The education system and the degradation of family values are primary contributors here.

2. Technology, the media, and pop culture promote and reinforce selfishness.

3. Society and government are warped by special interest groups and a flawed legal system.

These three reasons, and the institutional and societal elements that feed into them, explain how we got to our current state. I am sure there are others, but I firmly believe that these elements, which are intertwined, have had the most profound effect on the degradation of our society. The combination of these elements is the feeding mechanism for most of the others.

Lack of Foundation

As Florida Gators quarterback, Tim Tebow led his team to two national championships and won the Heisman Trophy in 2007. He's widely considered a legend in college football. But he also left his impact in other ways such as prompting an NCAA ban on symbols and messages in the black paint players wear under their eyes. Tebow, of course, was filling his black paint patches with Bible verses.

Tebow is very religious, which he demonstrated through his actions both on and off the football field. Although athletes commonly thank God in press interviews, Tebow took it a bit further. Beyond the scripture painted under his eyes, he famously took a knee in prayer to celebrate a touchdown during his NFL stint with the Denver Broncos, once again using his platform as a football hero to make a public statement about his values. And during the 2010 Super Bowl, he and his mother starred in an anti-abortion commercial by the conservative Christian group Focus on the Family.

The backlash to his displays of spirituality was brutal. Nielsen Sports found that the public began associating Tebow with negative phrases like "religious nut job." While still in college, he faced an inappropriate press question about his sex life. And as he failed to perform in the NFL and moved on to a minor league baseball career, which he genuinely seems to relish, press and social media commentators have taken delight in numerous and oddly personal attacks.

But why? Tebow is either thanking God for his accomplishments, promoting his genuine moral beliefs, or praying for help on the field. And regardless of whether you agree that abortion is wrong, making that commercial was a clear act of moral courage.

It's the same with Colin Kaepernick. As quarterback for the San Francisco 49ers, Kaepernick started an NFL player movement to call attention to racial injustice and police brutality. At the outset, he demonstrated this by sitting during the national anthem.

Nate Boyer, who had made multiple warzone deployments as a U.S. Army Green Beret and played in one NFL off-season game for the Seattle Seahawks, treasured his Kaepernick-signed football with the message "God Bless Our Troops." But he was disappointed and angry over Kaepernick's action. In an open letter published in the *Army Times*, Boyer wrote to Kaepernick as an unabashed fan struggling to be open to the protest's message. "Overcoming racism at home is a slow process, and we still have a long way to go, but most of us are trying," Boyer wrote. "That's what sets us apart from so many other places."

Kaepernick reached out to Boyer, and they met in the lobby of the team's hotel one day ahead of a 49ers game in San Diego. Boyer explained that a lot of people wouldn't be able to understand the message behind the gesture simply because it takes place during the anthem. He suggested Kaepernick kneel rather than sit.

Kaepernick then welcomed Boyer onto the field during the anthem at that San Diego game. Kaepernick kneeled on one knee, but Boyer stood, hand over heart. The gesture was an attempt by both men to communicate that they don't agree on everything, but that they are unified in Kaepernick's right to protest and his underlying message.

The involvement of a military hero did nothing to temper the public backlash. Boos erupted in the stadium. Social media was rife with claims that Kaepernick was unpatriotic and anti-military. President Donald Trump called for protesting players to be fired.

Kaepernick wasn't fired, but he was often benched. Still, he told the media that he'd be selfish to give up the protests at this point. He argued that the protest was more important than football. After the 2017 season, he opted out of his 49ers contract.

As of publication of this book, he continues to be a free agent. In September 2018, Nike chose Kaepernick to star in a major ad campaign marking the 30th anniversary of the company's "Just Do It" slogan. Again, the backlash came hard, with people burning Nike gear across the country. In my own neck of the woods, the mayor of Kenner, La., Ben Zahn, issued a policy forbidding youth recreation leagues from purchasing the company's gear (although he has since rescinded the policy).

Early indications show sales on the rise for Nike. Eleven days following the campaign's Sept. 3 release, Nike's stock closed at an all-time high. And the brand gained 170,000 new Instagram followers, significantly widening their audience for future marketing messages.

Who knows if this positive business trajectory will continue? For my purposes, it doesn't really matter. As I say repeatedly throughout this book, the Give a Damn philosophy won't always lead to success in stocks, on Instagram, or in revenue. But it will lead to the kind of success that matters to the human spirit. And that, I believe, is what is happening for both Kaepernick and Tebow.

Even if you disagree with the message underlying these players' public demonstrations or the way they chose to communicate them, both athletes displayed a clear commitment to moral integrity with the risks they took. And moral integrity, whether based on love of God or community or some other love greater than self, is a critical foundation for living a Give a Damn life.

Why should anyone be upset by someone bowing down to give thanks or call for change? These players' actions are not being directed at anyone personally, but people act like this is the case, and therefore they find the behavior offensive. No one should be offended by Tebow praying or Kaepernick taking a knee. Again, you don't have to agree with the messages, but people who are offended by this and try to do something to prevent it from happening are part of a bigger problem.

I know less about Kaepernick as a person, but I know that Tebow has no ulterior motive. In fact, it seems as though most of the controversy surrounding Tebow is the fact that he is one of the most uncontroversial athletes on the planet. He has no major vices, no criminal record, and practices the values that he preaches. It is as if he is holding up a mirror of what society could or should be, and those on the other side don't like what they see. Think about it.

Religion is a great foundation for building altruism and integrity. In fact, people who are religious live almost four years longer than those who have no religious affiliation, says a study from the Ohio State University. The study of more than 1,000 obituaries found the boost remained even after taking into account gender and marital status. "Religious affiliation had nearly as strong an effect on longevity as gender does, which is a matter of years of life," said lead author Laura Wallace.

Whether you're Christian, Jewish, Muslim, Buddhist, or follow another peace-loving religion, religion can be a powerful and positive influence on character. Spirituality helps us to be selfless—both inside and out—in a way that secular logic doesn't. Why is this a bad thing? It's not! But religion is fading from public life.

In the United States, we can no longer openly practice our religious beliefs, because, as Tebow demonstrated, doing so might offend others. Why? Because people think it is directly targeted at them and therefore take it personally. This could not be further from the truth. Or maybe it's just because they want the publicity and with today's social media it is a lot easier to get. Certain individuals and factions want to take the word "God" out of our society at every chance they get.

Religious expression should not be considered offensive. If God helps you give a damn in everyday life, then it's a matter of integrity. You should be free to take Him wherever you go. And it's a matter of moral courage that you must act in accordance with your conscience. For some players it's enough to just thank God in an interview. For Tebow, it's not.

Religion generally helps us to care for others and do the right thing. I also believe that it's possible to express religion in popular culture and professional life in ways that show empathy and respect for people who don't belong to the same religion. Trying to force someone to believe in a particular religion is a different story.

But, as Kaepernick demonstrates, Give a Damn has no religious boundaries. His message is not based on love of God, but rather love for people who he believes face injustice. Kaepernick shows that the Give a Damn movement is available to anyone. I personally believe, however, that it can be much more difficult to jumpstart your journey of change without a spiritual foundation, especially if you risk incurring the kind of backlash that these two NFL quarterbacks have experienced.

I'll discuss the concept of higher loves more in the next chapter. For now, I'll just say that, although religion can be a powerful guide, there are other forces that can reinforce and shape you.

The memory of a loving mother's guidance—and belief that she is always watching—can serve as that instinctual emotional support. The active support of a mentor can also do the trick. Or the broader Give a Damn herd can help you along your journey.

Toxic Reinforcements

I basically grew up in technology. I started my career at IBM in the 1980s, when the company was helping to revolutionize the use of personal computers, supermarket checkouts, personal banking, and telecommunications. In that decade, IBM took its first personal computer to market and began experimenting with network computing.

It was an exciting time. I got to see firsthand how technology could give people the ability to be more productive and get things done faster. I loved working in tech because it was constantly evolving and changing—and changing fast.

Years later, I helped start and sell an internet services provider in the early days of the World Wide Web, then helped play a major role in elevating Louisiana's status as a technology hub through my role as president of the Louisiana Technology Council. In that position, I had a chance to take a stand against corruption while also promoting the local business community. And technology played a major role in both of these efforts.

As I mentioned in the last chapter, the LTC project team was concerned by our finding that someone had deleted the New Orleans mayor and CIO's mailboxes. We considered, however, that the disappearance of this data might have been unintentional.

To see if they had been damaged by run-of-the-mill server problems, we restored and opened several mailboxes. Most came back with nothing but minor issues. These other users' restored mailboxes included deleted messages, sent messages, and calendar items. But this was not the case with the mailboxes of the mayor and CIO.

That's when we brought in specialized file recovery and undelete tools, such as Eseutil and Exmerge. When the city's main server ran out of space to process data, we brought in a computer with a 1.5-terabyte drive to run these tools. They all verified the same fact: on May 5, 2009, at 1:32 p.m., shortly after our first work call with the city, 22 gigabytes of data were deliberately deleted from the mail store.

And this message deletion was no simple process. It's not like when you or I delete an email, sending it to the trash folder, where it can easily be found. This had been a specially implemented task involving knowledge that only a systems administrator or another high-level IT technician could possess. It would have required external drive space and a sophisticated tool, such as Exmerge.

Once the technology tools opened our eyes, we had a major decision to make: Should we go public with our findings? After consulting legal counsel and the LTC board, we decided to go public with our general findings without providing the actual data. On June 23, we sent the recovered data—via a 670-megabyte .pst file (a file format used to store copies of messages, calendar events, and other items within Microsoft email systems)—to our contact at city hall.

On that same day, Christopher Reade at Carrollton Technology Partners, one of the companies working on the contract, and the city hall recipient of the file had a meeting. It was a candid discussion about the irregularities we found while recovering the data:

- On May 5, 2009, 22 gigabytes of email and other items for rnagin@mnomail.com were removed from a city hall database.

- The mayor's email prior to February 2009 couldn't be found anywhere—not on two restored versions of the new server's information store, and not in the mayor's then-current mailbox. It just didn't exist. Evidence showed that it had been there at some point.

- The mayor's then-current inbox was not storing sent emails. And they weren't being stored in any alternative way on the Microsoft Exchange email system used by the Nagin administration. They were being sent and then deleted at the same time.

On the morning of June 29, 2009, I notified the city via regular mail, email, and fax of our intention to go public on July 1 at 3 p.m. But I didn't hear from them until 30 minutes before the deadline. At that point, they told me over the phone that they didn't mind me going public with our results, just that they wanted to know what they were.

I was taken aback by this statement because the in-person meeting, postal mail, fax, and email all made it clear what we were going to announce. Clearly, it was time to move forward. We contacted the FBI. Then we proceeded with the press conference.

This story shows the role technology can play in sniffing out corruption. It can be an extremely positive influence on society. Technology can be helpful, but it can also have a dark side. In fact, a big reason for modern society's lack of care for others has been the advent and use of technology.

Now, you might say that technology, especially social media and mobile apps, has allowed us to communicate with more people than ever before. In one sense, this is true. And yet our interpersonal skills have suffered more than ever before.

With advances in technology, we can do things faster. But this speed advantage, too, comes at a behavioral cost. We have become fixated on the idea of instant gratification. We want what we want when we want it, and that "when" is usually right away! People seek immediate information via text and the internet, and as long as that information is fast, its accuracy is secondary.

Furthermore, face-to-face human interaction has decreased immensely due to the rapid onslaught of technology and the devices that we use every day. One of the biggest problems today is the decline of direct face-to-face interaction between people.

Instead of calling someone, you send a text. I have friends who tell me they would rather text than talk on the phone. Instead of writing someone, you send an email. These shortcuts shortchange personal interactions. Communication through email and texting can also be misinterpreted. It is easier to avoid an uncomfortable situation through email or text, but, in general, it is more effective and satisfying to deal with difficult situations directly via face-to-face communication.

Although talking on the phone isn't face-to-face, isn't verbal communication better than sending a text when it comes to interacting with someone? It's more personal. Many expressions are conveyed through vocal tone, or even pauses in speech, that are lost in text messages.

Society has become so technology-driven and things have become so automated that we don't have that human touch like we did before. Our communication standards are declining. Spelling and grammar no longer matter, and you can say pretty much whatever you want, as long as you insert a "jk," "lol," or smile emoji at the end of a statement.

Worst of all, this increase in digital communication makes it much easier for people to avoid real-world social interaction. The balance of interaction in society has tipped to greater communication with others, but at the expense of direct personal contact. Our interactions with others are increasing in quantity but are declining in quality.

This is a special problem among our youth because young people have had less time to practice important communications skills. We should be doing everything we can to support a child's social and emotional skills, as educators call them. These skills include their ability to feel empathy, control their behavior, and build relationships. Social-emotional skills are a critical tool for success in life.

But research shows that screen time can interrupt the process of learning and growing these skills. The American Academy of Pediatrics said in its 2016 policy statement, "Media and Young Minds," that television viewing in early childhood is strongly associated with social-emotional delays. And the statement expressed concern about the fact that devices showing any kind of content can now be taken anywhere.

The "Nielsen Total Audience Report" for the first quarter of 2018 found that young adults spend almost half of their time consuming media on various digital platforms. Of course, that's the most of any generation that Nielsen has ever measured. Almost a third of this media time is with apps and the internet via smartphones.

Many young people spend their time sharing selfies with hundreds of "friends" on a myriad of social media sites. I worry that if you reduce the desire for someone to interact directly with people in society, you reduce their ability to care or think about others. Whether in the form of obsessively updating profile pictures, texting through family dinners, or being absorbed in violent video games, all this new technology is taking its toll on social-emotional skills like empathy and a general concern for others.

And guess what? Lack of empathy in individuals may be directly correlated to criminal acts, especially violent ones. The Konrath analysis noted that, although violent criminal acts declined during the first decade of this century, violence toward stigmatized, marginalized, or otherwise defenseless groups (such as homeless people, perceived immigrants, and LGBT individuals) rose significantly. What will an increase in violence and a lack of empathy look like in 20 years when our current youth are adults?

And the problem doesn't just stem from the devices and platforms through which we consume this content. Smartphones, social media platforms, and all the other technology systems are just content delivery vehicles. Equally important is the message being delivered by this content—and the popular culture that's driving it. Today's audiences are obsessed with the Kardashians and other reality—or what I would call unreality—TV shows with little substance and a lot of shock or wow factors built in.

Seemingly the message received by most everyone, whether young or old, is that honest hard work is just too much work! Today, many of the messages we receive from the media do anything *but* support a Give a Damn attitude. Entertainment is designed to contain so-called unbelievable moments or provide cheap laughs rather than provoke thought and reflection.

Social media is playing a big role in all of this, and we are all complicit. We are no longer just consumers of content anymore. We are creators, too! And all of us who generate content online, on TV, in the movies, and in music need to realize and understand the responsibility we have to clear our children's path of toxic obstacles.

Too many young people are captivated by songs about designer clothes and private jets, the opulent Instagram feeds of their favorite celebrities, and the million-dollar mansions of reality TV. They associate these lavish displays of wealth with respect and power, and they don't realize that most of it is fantasy.

The media—especially social media—constantly feeds this kind of narrative to our youth. Viewers only see the end result and they have no idea that success doesn't happen overnight. They rarely see that success is the result of hard work and not just intricate production techniques that go into creating an image of extreme wealth. As such, they want instant gratification and aspire to grab a piece of the pie as quickly and easily—and falsely—as they imagine their favorite stars have done.

It's a bad message, but it sure has a major impact on ratings. Ah yes, ratings. Also likes, tweets and retweets, follows, and more. More attention, more dollars, more profits. And usually at the expense of doing the right thing. Some would say that people who watch TV and browse social media know that it's fantasy. That may be true for adults, but not for younger kids. Children are so impressionable, and what impression is all of this giving them? Popular culture in its current form teaches nothing or very little about how to give a damn.

Sitcoms about model families and groups of close friends have been replaced with scantily dressed pop stars' videos, trashy reality TV shows, and social media content from overpaid athletes who care only for themselves and who are often above reproach. Our role models today in pop music, television, movies, fashion, and professional sports suggest that the way to be truly successful and happy in life is to be very thin, have multiple houses, drive fast cars, engage in promiscuous behavior, wear a lot of expensive flashy jewelry or clothing, and abuse drugs and alcohol.

To be in and out of rehab is now a sign that you have arrived! The people that our children look up to and the media that surrounds them suggests that bad language and a self-absorbed lifestyle will get you lots of attention—never mind if it's negative!

Certainly, there are celebrities, artists, and athletes who use their fame to raise money and awareness for charities and other worthy causes. Many adopt needy children and make very positive changes in our world. They do their best to carry themselves well and deliver a positive message. There are a number of them, but how often do they get recognized compared to the celebrities who are misbehaving?

Way too often, these good deeds take a back seat to the more risky, rude, and obnoxious actions of many self-absorbed celebrities with seemingly insatiable egos. We all know there are exceptions to everything, but these elements seem to be more and more commonplace than ever before. We no longer have the many positive role models that once taught us how to give a damn.

Our remaining positive role models often do not receive the same amount of advertising money or media coverage than less scrupulous stars do because it won't bring in ratings, thus hindering their success. Scandalous behavior attracts more attention, which is exactly what media moguls want: sensationalism. It turns into ratings, which in turn pays the bills!

We see individualistic, disrespectful, and even criminal behavior all over TV, radio, and social media outlets. And this behavior seems to be encouraged because it's perceived as funny or clever. We laugh these things off instead of being horrified, making excuses like, "You've got to hand it to him—he got away with it," or "It's not real, it's only TV."

This obsession with fame has shifted to a much darker side as well. Our political leaders engage in sexual misconduct, fraud, and theft. They lie and cheat and lie some more. And, unbelievably, they get re-elected. News programs are full of stories about shootings in schools, movie theatres, and malls. Many of these shooters are seeking the news coverage and notoriety that they see as the ultimate achievement.

This is like a cancer, breeding upon itself. Incomprehensible actions that show up in the media are seeping their way into and engulfing our society, and are, sadly, being accepted. It is disgusting and appalling. To me, these toxic reinforcements from technology, media, and pop culture aren't a joke. They're a major impediment to change. And there are already enough of those toxic reinforcements blocking our path to a better way.

These elements also feed into each other. With the combination of technology, media, and pop culture, our children have more access to negative behaviors than ever before. The internet and television provide a constant stream of activities related to famous people and their inappropriate behaviors. And the ordinary citizens that we choose to promote to celebrity status in viral videos and reality shows are generally the ones with the least amount of education, manners, and class.

Regardless of whether you are a singer with a global audience or a small business owner with a neighborhood clientele, whatever your actions are, they will affect both you and others. This is always the case, because we do not operate in a vacuum. Your thinking should be based on the effect that your actions or words will have on others. You set the tone with a Give a Damn attitude. The effect of whatever you do might not be immediate, but it will certainly have an impact on you at some point in the future.

Special Interest Over Public Interest

The earliest days of the United States were stained by war, human slavery, and other tragedies. But they were also marked by the wisdom of our founding fathers. Their leadership exhibited long-term thinking and collaboration for the public interest, something lacking in politics today. The Constitution clearly shows that our founding fathers were more focused on others than themselves. They were concerned with morals and values, and they were thinking about future generations.

But as time moves on, these founding beliefs seem to be changing with the masses or are twisted to accommodate people's self-interests. People today are often so caught up in furthering their personal agenda that they impose their own causes onto others. They say that they are making changes to benefit society as a whole when we know darn well that is not the case. Usually their changes are based on their best interests or the best interests of only a few.

Gun laws are a good example. I don't believe the founding fathers could have ever envisioned an automatic rifle that can shoot 400 rounds per minute. And yet, special interest groups have found a way to keep these types of assault weapons legal by using the Constitution to their advantage and to the detriment of others. Laws have been interpreted in a way that allows these harmful weapons to be accessible by hobbyists and criminals alike.

Answer me this question: What would be the main purpose for an individual to have this kind of weapon? Common sense tells me that no one can think of one good or legitimate reason to have this type of weapon in their possession, other than for military use. The right to bear arms is a constitutional right, and I agree with that. But not any type of weapon that is designed for mass killing.

Although our legal and governing institutions have had a long and successful history, I believe they have veered off their path in terms of what they are supposed to do for society.

Special interest groups were originally designed to assist marginalized groups of our population who were not given a voice or permitted equal rights. Without someone speaking up for minority groups, women might not have been granted the right to vote and we might still have racially segregated schools. These special interests are important, as are many others.

However, special interest groups have now become so prevalent and powerful in our political system that sometimes the needs and interests of a few individuals outweigh the needs and interests of the majority of citizens, to the point that the entire system is dysfunctional or paralyzed.

We need to change our mindset and change it now. Yes, in a society where the foundations of education, faith, and family values are degraded—where it is acceptable to be impatient, rude, selfish, drunk, lazy, and ignorant—it will be a real challenge to incite change. But, it is not impossible.

The next six chapters detail additional institutions in our society where contributing factors are feeding into a don't Give a Damn mentality. After identifying these problems, I will offer solutions in the final chapters of this book.

Read on to find out why our lack of a Give a Damn attitude is killing society and what we can do as individuals working together to fix it. Again,

Individually you make a difference,

Collectively we change the world!

Chapter 3 – Giving a Damn Starts at Home

My kids sometimes used to say to me, "Dad, all you think about is money!" Later in life I admitted, to my ultimate disappointment, that they were probably right. However, there really is another side to the story. I worked hard to have enough money to provide for my family and my kids.

Most kids don't realize how much money goes into meeting their wants and needs. Providing them with food, shelter, entertainment, and a great education—among many other things—isn't free! And during periods when I was really too focused on money, I suffered the consequences because of it.

After my first post-IBM experience and when the startup world went south (a story for another day), I got intrigued by this new thing called the internet, which I really knew nothing about. I wrote a business plan for an internet service provider. I financed the business through credit cards, and the next thing I knew I was helping to operate a new startup out of a garage.

I knew the exit strategy one day would be to sell this business to a much larger and well-financed player in the marketplace. To make this plan work, we were focused on creating as much value for the company as possible. It's the typical Silicon Valley mindset: grow really big, really fast. But as a result, I lost that balance between family and work.

You can probably predict what happened—I know I should have, but I was blind in many ways. My marriage suffered. I got separated a couple of times, then ultimately divorced. My relationship with my kids suffered, too.

Sure, money should be a factor when you have to earn a living and meet the needs of your family, but it's your relationship with them that is most important. I regret the times when I lost sight of this.

Some of the most basic challenges to adopting a Give a Damn attitude and lifestyle stem from the earliest issues we are exposed to as children: our relationships with our immediate family, the presence of religion in our lives, and our personal dynamic with money. Parents must grapple with these issues in the home, or else they will haunt us and our children for the rest of our lives. Here, we will explore the problems that arise within our homes that we can only solve through changing our own habits, mindsets, and attitudes.

Wealth and Family

If you reflect on your life, would a bigger house make you happier? You might initially say yes, but in the long term, probably not. Would a better-paying job make you happier? Same thought process, but probably not. Even if these things did make you happier for a short time, you would eventually want more. That is the nature of material things—there is always something better.

Some interesting new insights have come out of the research lab of Paul K. Piff, assistant professor of psychology at the University of California Irvine who has long looked at the intersection of money and happiness. Past research has shown that lower-class people (such as those without a college education) have worse health, experience more social exclusion, and even report lower well-being. But Piff's research seems to turn that on its head.

Piff's 2017 study was the first to test the relationship between social class and multiple aspects of happiness—including love, pride, contentment, and compassion. The study looked at a nationally representative sample of more than 1,500 adults.

His team found that self-centered positive emotions may be more strongly associated with upper-class versus lower-class individuals. But other-centered emotions, like compassion and love, may be strongly associated with people normally considered to fall into a lower socioeconomic class.

"Turning to the association between social class and other-oriented positive emotion, social class negatively predicted compassion, indicating that lower class individuals reported more caring for others than upper class participants, as prior research has shown," the study said. "We also found that social class negatively predicted love—the first demonstration that lower class individuals are more prone to positive feelings of attachment and emotional intimacy."

So, take care! Can money really be the root of emotional evil? It's wonderful to be successful, but don't lose sight of your love and compassion for others. These are key ingredients for a happy life.

Regardless of what the research says, common sense says that we couldn't have been put on this earth merely to amass wealth. Yet some people think this way. People who are focused on making money are, in general, constantly driven by two thoughts: "What's in it for me?" and "How can I get ahead?" This pursuit of status and wealth is what sometimes overwhelmingly shapes people's life decisions. I thought this way for a time and it affected my relationships with my family and, to a lesser degree, with my friends.

But my focus on money wasn't all selfish. I wanted my children to become independent and responsible adults. Once they reach a certain age, our children ultimately have to take full responsibility for their lives and must fend for themselves. Having them fall down without helping them get back can be painful. But we just can't continue to give without our kids taking responsibility, no matter how hard that might be. Otherwise, they will never learn.

So, after they reached their early 20s, if my kids lived with me, I charged them rent. What I was really trying to teach them was a continuance of gaining more responsibility as they became adults. They needed to learn to be on their own (whether in my house or renting an apartment) and to contribute to society.

I wanted them to find a means of supporting themselves, even if it was difficult at times for them. I wanted my children to lead purposeful lives and not give them a free ride. I wanted them to know that life is not always easy.

I can't really blame my kids for disagreeing with this philosophy of mine. Being my children wasn't always easy for them. I remember one time when they were particularly affected by my work. It was an extension of the Nagin corruption story that opened this book.

It was 2:30 p.m. on the Tuesday before the Louisiana Technology Council planned to go public with our findings. Of particular concern to us were those irregularities we encountered during our work recovering data from the Nagin administration's computer servers.

I was in a meeting that afternoon with a client when I suddenly received a call from my son asking me if I had changed the door locks to the house. I was confused and asked him, "Why would I do that and not tell you about it?" He stated that he had tried to insert the key into all eight of my exterior locks and it would not go in. Now I was even more confused.

I was about to finish my meeting, so I told him that I would arrive home in about an hour. When I got there, I called the police. A single squad car showed up and a police officer briefly spoke to me and then went back to her car. She was in her car for about 30 minutes speaking to people on her phone. Suddenly, I had around 10 police officers investigating the entire exterior of my house.

Crime scene investigators dusted for fingerprints, removed one of my exterior door locks for evidence, and more. It turned out that someone had actually squirted superglue into all of my exterior door locks. Fortunately, one lock was not fully compromised and we were able to get into the house. For more than four years, I had lived in this quiet neighborhood without such incidents, and there haven't been any since. And this all happened the day before we were to go public with our findings about the Nagin administration server.

By that time, I had been divorced, and my youngest daughter (who was about 12 years old) was living with me. She became quite frightened. I told her that if it made her feel more comfortable, she should spend time with her mom until this whole thing blew over.

For my part, I slept well that night. I knew that through this whole ordeal I was doing the right thing. To this day, we do not know who compromised my house. We can only assume and imagine.

This is a story of a family being under great stress due to a parent's work. Usually, the consequences are not so dramatic, and the stakes at work aren't so high. Most of the time it's just a matter of lost connections and weakened relationships due to a lack of balance and priorities.

Over the years, I have worked hard to enhance, and at times repair, my relationship with my children. I have made a point to spend more time with them. I purposefully organized regular family functions with them, and our communication has improved. Technology actually played a role, as we use emails and text messages to augment our in-person communication. But I have also apologized and put my love for them down in multiple handwritten letters and greeting cards.

My children are independent adults now with good jobs. But more importantly, they demonstrate accountability and respect toward others. I'm so proud of them, and I'm grateful for our relationships, which continue to strengthen and I believe we all enjoy.

I made a mistake, and everyone has in some way. Most of us are given another chance, just like my kids did for me. I don't dwell on not being a better father for them earlier in life because parenting is a tough job. They are really outstanding Give a Damn people and now I hope I'm the father they deserve.

A Higher Love

Early in our children's lives, we need to set a foundation for a proper hierarchy of priorities. So, if amassing wealth isn't the highest priority (which it should not be), what is? The Give a Damn philosophy offers a simple answer: serving others.

Giving service should be a major emphasis, and part of this emphasis can be spiritual. Isn't serving others part of what God wants us to do?

Give a Damn has no religious boundaries. It doesn't matter whether you are Catholic, Protestant, Buddhist, Jewish, Muslim, or any other religion. One doesn't even need a religion to incorporate Give a Damn into their lives. A person does not need religion at all to have integrity, values, and a moral disposition or courage.

However, it helps to believe that your maker, whomever you choose that to be, is always watching you. Still, there are people who don't think this way because they don't believe in God. Maybe, as an alternative, it's your mom or a significant mentor that can be the second strongest motivator for making sure you always give a damn.

When I first got into motivational speaking, my first corporate audience was the IT department (40+ employees) of a major organization in New Orleans. The technology leader, Ruark Chick, was moved by some of the Give a Damn values—especially accountability and integrity.

These concepts were already integral parts of his philosophy and leadership style. He believes that integrity, trust, and honesty are the "nucleus around which everything is built in an effective team environment."

So, Chick brought me in to give a secular Give a Damn presentation to his team at their annual IT summit, and he bought copies of the first edition of the book for everyone. They made "Give a Damn" their team motto, using it not only for every project at the summit, but also returning to it throughout the entire year when they hit a tough spot. I was grateful for the opportunity, and it cemented my desire to motivate more crowds by speaking about the Give a Damn philosophy.

Chick and I agree that the Give a Damn motivation can come from a variety of secular sources—a "gumbo," as he calls it, of positive influences in our lives. For example, Chick developed the principles that have guided his professional success from his parents, from the hardships he's had to overcome, and from influential people, such as teachers and friends. This nutritious gumbo shaped Chick's personal integrity and values.

"It boils down to 'do what you say and say what you do.' Our words and actions should always match," Chick told me in an interview. "And when people see that, they trust what you say. They know you're doing what you do because of a strategy, a vision. They know you can be counted on for whatever is needed to get a project done or an issue resolved."

I love Chick's concept of a "gumbo of influences," especially the valuable influence that the integrity and values of positive people can have on others. You must assume that your mother or someone else vastly important to you is always watching everything you say, think, and do. Who wants to disappoint mom? If you think your mother is watching, you will most likely do the right thing, correct? Everyone has had, or does have, a mom or role model. If this is what it takes for you to give a damn, I am all for it.

Think about it this way. If you are comfortable with going public with any decision that you make or action that you take, then it is a sure bet that you are doing the right thing. You are not keeping anything hidden, so to speak, and you are setting an example for others to follow. If you are willing to conduct your actions in an open manner, then it's a pretty safe bet that you do give a damn.

So, mom or a mentor can serve as your stand-in for a spiritual creator, at least until you have developed your inner Give a Damn compass. However, I am going to, again, get a bit religious here because I believe it drives home a key point.

Having some kind of higher love in your life is a key part of the Give a Damn philosophy because love shapes our attitudes and actions. A person driven by lower loves, such as self-interest and money, will treat other human beings in a dramatically different way than a person driven by higher loves, such as community or, in my case, a belief in God.

I am a fairly religious person. I pray regularly and also try to go to church every week, primarily to learn something new and to reinforce my beliefs. If you think about it, the Bible is really the closest thing to a Give a Damn book. It is not the foundation for this book, but it could be.

The Bible points out (1 Corinthians 10:24), "Nobody should seek his own good but the good of others." Therefore, we should not be conceited, provoking, and envious of each other; rather, we should be kind and compassionate to one another. Forgiving and understanding translates to someone who gives a damn.

Often, we subconsciously want others to give a damn about us. Yet when it comes to our own thoughts and actions, we don't give a damn because we are too wrapped up in a self-serving attitude. People want others to think of them, but at the same time, they think about themselves more than others without even realizing it.

Matthew 7:12 states, "Do unto others as you would have others do unto you." This describes people who give a damn. And even if we don't follow the golden rule in our initial action, there's still an opportunity to do so after the fact. So, when you make a mistake, no matter how trivial, admit it. Whatever you do, don't try to find a way to justify the mistake by blaming someone or something that happened.

It is also written in the Bible (Luke 6:38), "Give and it will be given to you," which means that the more we put into something the more we'll get out of it. At the same time, however, we should not expect to get anything in return for our giving. That's where people get it wrong. In reality, we will always get something in return! The problem is that people's thought process is often the reverse of what it should be because of their "What's in it for me?" attitude.

Most have heard the phrase, "You reap what you sow." This mainstream expression, of course, stems from a verse in Galatians (6:7). It's a good guiding philosophy, but we should never *expect* to reap a reward for selfless acts. That is the problem with today's society though. More and more people only do well if they foresee an immediate return or some type of benefit. Otherwise, they are probably very reluctant to do anything at all. We should do things out of the goodness of our hearts by helping others and then leave it in God's or someone else's hands for the "reap what you sow" reward. God will eventually reward you, but you should never expect it.

We need to humble ourselves when dealing with others, and not be misled by our pride. It is written in the Bible, "Whoever exalts himself will be humbled, and he who humbles himself will be exalted" (Matthew 23:12). Never let your ego convince you that you are better or more righteous than another. In a similar vein, the Bible says, "Therefore let us stop passing judgment on one another. Instead, make up your mind not to put any stumbling block or obstacle in your brother's way" (Romans 14:13).

Always thank God for His goodness. Anytime something good happens, big or little, give God or someone else thanks. "Lord, thank you for that special moment." "Lord, thank you for that idea." "Lord, thank you for making me a servant." "Lord, thank you for helping me to help others." If you do this, you are going to come into more of God's goodness—and thus, your own goodness—through your Give a Damn actions. His blessings are going to come to you more than ever before. God will help you open up doors. He will help turn negative situations around. Give a Damn people get ready, because something good is coming your way! You're going to fulfill your God-given destiny because He never forsakes those who give a damn!

A friend of mine went through a painful divorce after nearly 20 years of marriage. She had married young and had spent most of her adult life raising her children. When her marriage ended, she struggled to find her own identity, separate from that as a wife and mother. She decided to make a career change and eventually felt called to move to another state to pursue another job opportunity.

She believed the new job would enable her to make a big difference in the lives of others. To do this, she gave up her house and belongings, took a cut in pay, and left her close friends and children (who supported her in her major life decision).

In doing so, she made an unbelievable leap of faith. She did what few people have the courage to do, especially when it came to her children. She planned to make sure that she supported and visited them often. She gave up financial security and possessions in the hopes of having a more purpose-driven life. She put her faith in God and trusted that by doing good things for others and her family, her needs would be provided for.

I recall that she once said to me, her eyes smiling, "I think I know the secret. I have learned that there is little I can do to make myself truly happy. I must depend on God to make me happy and to meet my needs. When I have a need, I have to trust God to supply according to His riches."

She went on to tell me that most of the time she doesn't need half of what she thinks she needs. But if she gives a damn and does all that she can for others, she realized that God will never let her down. She had learned the secret—to give a damn—and that made her happy.

I'll close this section with one final story of a parent who knew the value of a higher love. David Brooks' bestseller *The Road to Character* is based on Jewish interpretation of the two accounts of creation in the book of Genesis.

In a chapter on Ida Stover Eisenhower (yes, the mother of President Dwight Eisenhower), Brooks writes of her parenting strategy:

> The tender character-building strategy is based on the idea that we can't always resist our desires, but we can change and reorder our desires by focusing on our higher loves. Focus on your love for your children. Focus on your love of country. Focus on your love for the poor and downtrodden. Focus on your love of your hometown or alma mater. To sacrifice for such things is sweet. It feels good to serve your beloved. Giving becomes cheerful giving because you are so eager to see the things you love prosper and thrive.

So religion—whichever peace-loving religion you choose—provides one of the most powerful forms of a higher love, a source of strength in adopting and sticking to a Give a Damn attitude.

But I also believe that values, moral integrity, and lasting change can come from orienting yourself toward any number of other higher loves.

Tradition Lost

A mother was preparing pancakes for her sons, Kevin, 5, and Ryan, 3. The boys began to argue over who would get the first pancake. Their mother saw the opportunity for a moral lesson. She said, "If Jesus were sitting here, He would say, 'Let my brother have the first pancake, I can wait.'" Kevin turned to his younger brother and said, "Ryan, you be Jesus!" Sure, this sermon joke is supposed to be funny, but the message is clear.

In perpetuating a don't Give a Damn mentality, the largest issue may be found in the waning of traditional values. People are brought up in multiple environments that just don't teach how to give a damn. If you don't understand the things you should and should not do, how can you change?

Over the past 20 to 30 years, parents have become less concerned with teaching their children values such as respect, responsibility, and common courtesy. They feel that they must put themselves and their work first in order to provide their families with food and shelter. But doing so can elevate money as a priority over serving others. And it can model this problematic attitude for a child.

I remember growing up how I wanted to be first in everything, especially over my twin sister. Most kids probably do the same because they don't know any better at a young age. For instance, my mom had a steak bone for a neighbor's dog, and my sister and I were fighting over who was going to give it to him. We were 8 years old at the time and we were both climbing concrete steps at the same time to get the bone.

My sister was ahead of me, so I pulled her down to get ahead. She landed on her chin and required six stitches. I should have let my sister give the dog the bone, and my opportunity would have come later.

Because I didn't give a damn, my sister got hurt. But at my age I did not know any better. It is natural for young children to exhibit selfish behavior, but our responsibility as parents is to lead by example and help children understand the importance—and the reward—of putting others first. If we don't teach our children this lesson early, society will certainly pay for it later.

Now contrast that story of my own childhood selfishness with a little boy who knew the importance of giving when it counts. Years ago, a friend worked as a volunteer at a hospital and got to know a little girl named Liz (not her actual name).

Liz was suffering from a rare and serious disease. Her only chance of recovery appeared to be a blood transfusion from her 5-year-old brother Oscar, who had miraculously survived the same disease and had developed the antibodies needed to combat the illness.

The doctor explained the situation to Oscar and asked him if he would be willing to give his blood to his sister. He hesitated only for only a moment before taking a deep breath and saying, "Yes, I'll do it if it will save her," my friend recalled. As the transfusion progressed, he lay in bed next to Liz and smiled.

But with the procedure complete, Oscar's face grew pale and his smile faded, my friend told me. He looked up at the doctor and asked with a trembling voice, "Will I start to die right away?" Confused, the doctor gave him a perplexed look. Then he realized that, being so young, Oscar had misunderstood the doctor; he thought he was going to have to give his sister all his blood to save her. This story shows how Give a Damn people always think about others before themselves—and how they're capable of learning these values from a very early age.

Although there are always challenges and difficulties in raising a child, we actually give a damn more for kids than anyone else. Why? We take care of children because they cannot fend for themselves and are still learning and developing.

Chivalry used to be a big part of family values in the past. I think it's on its way out or has been out for some time. Chivalry can be summed up as thinking of and doing things for other people, however small they might be. And it's not just a male thing, either. Chivalry is as easy as opening a car door for someone, getting up so that another person might sit down on a bus, letting someone get in an elevator before you, holding a door open, or helping someone walk across the street. These are simple and small gestures that show respect for other people, no matter who they are.

Another thing lost in today's society is the teaching of etiquette. Good and proper etiquette is a Give a Damn trait. What happened to the words "excuse me," "please," and "thank you?" These simple words are missing more and more from today's society. Parents can give a damn by teaching their children the value of doing the right thing at a very early age. And simply using these three phrases would be a huge step in the right direction.

Discussing these behaviors is important, but if we were to show children how to give a damn over and over again, it would become a learned response and an instinctive part of a child's wiring of the brain. Parents need to demonstrate through their own words and actions that wealth and status are earned and could possibly fade, but being a good person never does. It would be a gift to give to our children: our learned Give a Damn behavior.

The subconscious mind knows how to give a damn. We just don't execute it consciously. Can we teach ourselves and others how to give a damn? I think we can, and it's done most effectively through our actions. Instead of just telling our children to share and take turns and admonishing them with, "If you can't say anything nice, don't say anything at all," we have to show to our children that we *do* these good things. And we must point out the positive effects our actions have on others. People can learn to give a damn if they are simply aware of the positive effects it can have on people.

Some years ago, I volunteered to chair a $4 million capital campaign to help raise funds for the renovation of my children's church and school. What could I possibly get out of this? Nothing directly, but that wasn't the point. I wanted my kids to have the best education possible, and I knew I would meet a lot of nice and giving people along the way and make new friends. But I also knew that stepping into this role would show my children how to love something bigger than their own short-term interests.

Teaching moral lessons and modeling good behavior are both equally important, but I believe that consequences, even corporal punishment, can sometimes be helpful as well. This idea about child abuse has gone way too far. I am all about protecting children from being abused and there are certainly limits. However, there is a difference between child abuse and child punishment.

Spanking a child for doing something wrong is not child abuse, it's called a consequence for doing something wrong, also known as tough love. There are lots of ways, however, to demonstrate consequences. The Konrath team's review of parenting research noted that parents who promote empathy development are high in "other-oriented" punishment strategies, such as instructing a child to "imagine how he must feel."

The researchers also pointed to a study showing that adults had more empathy if their mothers had inhibited their aggression when they were children. It's our responsibility to shape our children's personalities at an early age, even if it doesn't always feel good in the moment.

Sadly, our version of tough but responsible love is basically gone. By the time children are 13 years old, their Give a Damn (or don't) mentality is probably already formed. Ideas and habits formed in response to our individual experiences as we grow up can be very difficult to change. Difficult—but not impossible! When parents exemplify a Give a Damn attitude, their actions rub off on their children, even if it might not seem apparent at first.

For example, I had a friend who was complaining to me about his lazy 22-year-old son who lived with him. He did laundry but only his own, he never cleaned up after himself, he took clean dishes out of the dishwasher but never emptied it completely, and he never cleaned his bathroom. The list went on.

I told my friend to use the Give a Damn approach toward his son, but not to the point where he would become submissive. I told him that it might take a while, but that the Give a Damn seed would germinate with time. Eventually it did, but not until his son was on his own.

I guess he finally realized that in order to really succeed in life, you need to give a damn on a consistent basis. And his father's demonstrations of hard work, commitment, ethics, and accountability had finally sprouted the seed in his own spirit and life.

Everyone has a Give a Damn seed inside. These seeds might take longer to germinate in some people than others. It just depends on the environment, past situations, learned behavior, and the amount of nurturing that the seeds receive. But the seed is there for germinating!

Unfortunately, modern society imposes a sharp cut-off between childhood and adulthood. Today, when a child hits 18, they are on their own. When I was 18, my parents were still very much involved with my life; they guided me, helped me get into college, helped me with medical issues, and much more. Once kids turn 18, parents cannot get information about their children without their children's permission, whereas 20 years ago it wasn't a problem.

My thought is that if parents declare a child on their tax return as a dependent and fully support them and their needs, then the parents should have access to their child's school and medical records, with or without the child's consent. If the child is totally on their own, parents don't need this information anyway. Society has created an environment in which parents cannot assist children like they used to.

People are brought up in multiple environments that just don't teach how to give a damn. Teaching behaviors like kindness, moral courage, and positivity should start at home and at the earliest age possible. It is what will eventually drive society.

It might be difficult to do at first, especially as an adult, but you have to start somewhere. This is not something that can be done overnight. You must take responsibility for your own actions and show that you can and will give a damn in everything that you say and do. You have to demonstrate it with your own words and actions.

If you really want to give a damn, you are going to need energy, compassion, and self-awareness to make it work. You will be amazed at the positive effect it will have on people and on you. It will rub off on others, especially your children. It will take time, but it's so important for this world. And we have to do it one person at a time.

Chapter 4 – Give a Darn at School

In 1975, I started to comb the pages of my first finance and management textbooks in a classroom at beautiful and historic Boston College. My alma mater gave me so much more than a degree. It gave me opportunities to dream big, take on responsibility, and experience the joy of working on real-world solutions.

In the mid 1970s, the whole country had been shaken by the energy crisis and the economic downturn that it caused. I wanted to do something to help. As a result, I founded a club called the Student Energy Commission. I put together a plan that I presented to the university for approval, and it was accepted. The plan was designed to reduce the school's energy consumption by creating awareness and therefore save the university money.

Boston College took a chance on me. The university gave me $2,500 to spend on implementing my plan. Our marketing efforts included stickers for light switches, costumed characters (Mr. Kill-A-Watt and DimIt DimWatt), an energy "fast" day, and a lights-off disco dance with glow sticks for lighting. We also created a T-shirt with the slogan, "Do it in the dark." Pretty risqué for a Jesuit school, don't you think? But they bought into my plan!

Boston College's gamble on my ideas paid off. The $2,500 investment resulted in $250,000 in energy savings over the academic year. And three years later, I walked away with an education worth ten times that amount.

I donate every year to my alma mater, but I should probably do more. Boston College and the Student Energy Commission were the springboard for my career and professional principles. I am forever shaped by the experiences I had there and the administration that believed in me.

Did you have a wonderful experience in school? Or did your high school, college, or grad school leave much to be desired? How did your education aid or hinder your social and emotional development? I'm aware and blessed that I'm one of the lucky ones. I've had great educational experiences and have been supported by so many people, including my most important mentor and teacher, my dad. Not everyone can say the same. This has huge implications for our society.

I think a lot of people don't give a damn because they just don't know any better. Perhaps they never had someone show interest in them or mentor them as I was mentored. They are unaware of their surroundings and how their actions might affect others. People don't realize the consequences of their actions, but it may not be entirely their fault. If you don't understand the things you should and should not be doing, if you can't grasp the meaning of integrity, how can you change?

It is a problem within our changing society that stems from our cultural environment and how our education system operates. There is just not enough focus on what it takes to be a quality human being, and there's not enough appreciation for the role that educators can play at all levels. Or maybe our schools are delivering the message, but it's just not sinking in. And maybe it's not sinking in because we are not emphasizing it enough.

Valuing Education

Many people take our education system for granted or don't perceive that it provides much value. This disregard for education is clearly illustrated by an example from the state I now call home, Louisiana. In 2002, citizens voted to amend our state constitution to cut sales taxes, which tend to hit poor people the hardest. This was called the Stelly Plan, after then-state Rep. Vic Stelly, and it eliminated sales taxes on food for home consumption and utilities.

To compensate for this revenue loss, the state legislature raised individual state income tax rates on higher-income earners. The result was a more progressive tax system based on the assumption that a stronger and steadier revenue growth model would develop over time.

By 2007, Louisiana lawmakers wanted to repeal the Stelly tax increase on these higher-income earners. Such a move, however, would have a devastating effect on higher education, seemingly always one of the sectors hit the hardest during a budget crisis in Louisiana.

There was a proposal to defer the repeal. Many people were totally against the deferral, including small businesses. But why? I really don't get it other than it being an example of pure self-centered thinking.

They were only thinking of themselves and the immediate benefit of more cash in their pockets. They were not thinking about how important education was for our state (let alone our country), especially when education quality is deteriorating at a rapid pace compared to other countries.

I argued against the repeal in front of about 40 people while presenting on behalf of the Louisiana Technology Council, stating that we really needed to improve the quality of education for our students. But most people were more concerned about what they could get back. The common cry was, "We already pay too much in taxes anyway!"

So, certain lawmakers, concerned more about votes than about the future of Louisiana's educational system, went along with the people. Isn't that what lawmakers are supposed to do? Yet common sense told me otherwise. The Stelly Plan was abolished, and almost a decade later, our state's higher education system faces its worst crisis ever. State support for colleges and universities has significantly declined, while students and families face almost a 100 percent increase in the burden of tuition and fees.

I was disturbed by the repeal because it really showed that people think, "What's best for me?" instead of what might be best for the state as a whole.

It's just part of a broader national story about how we fail to prioritize high-quality education. The quality of education is waning—both in character education and formal coursework. This stems from two sources.

One issue is the decreasing value that popular culture places on education. Instead, it elevates the ideal of an in-the-moment lifestyle, which places good times and risky actions over discipline and study. The second cause is the greed and mismanagement of voters and politicians alike, who seem to cut education funding more and more every year.

According to the Organisation for Economic Co-operation and Development's Better Life Index, which compares well-being across countries, in 2015, U.S. middle schoolers were in the lower middle scores for math, science, and reading. For adults, the scores in math were even worse, putting us behind all other nations except Spain and Italy! The difference between the United States and high-scoring countries, such as Finland, Japan, and Korea, is that these countries chose to increase funding for education instead of cutting it.

What's really interesting about those who prefer cutting education is their short-term thinking. Although they think they're saving money, a country's quality of education has a direct impact on its GDP. A quality education boosts both the productivity and cognitive skills of a population, leading to a more resilient and innovative workforce.

A more innovative workforce leads to greater progress in technology, which is a source of continuous economic growth for any country that can harness it. When you have quality education at every level, it's not just students who win, it's society as a whole.

K Through 12

A long time ago, I heard a song at my son's school that really provided an ah-ha moment for me. The lyrics went as follows:

> Make me a servant, humble and meek.
> Lord, let me lift up those who are weak.
> And may the prayer of my heart always be,
> Make me a servant, make me a servant,
> Make me a servant today.

If only we would wake up every morning with these words in mind and find a way to be of service to our fellow men and women. I hope that one day people's attitudes will change, and this book is my attempt to contribute to that change. At the end of the day, we are not put on earth for ourselves. We are here for each other and to serve each other in the best possible way we can. By serving others we serve ourselves. Just don't get it reversed.

The best and most effective way to start is to push for a better-educated society across all levels, and to start at an early age. It will take many, many years to change a society's mindset, but someone has to start the process. We need to have a much greater focus in our school systems on teaching the Give a Damn attitude (which, for those tender ears, I'll call Give a Darn in this chapter). When I say education, I mean two kinds: character and scholastic.

Ideally, we should teach our children to consider behaviors like service, positivity, courtesy, and honesty at an early age. I believe that teaching kids how to contribute to society—the real reason why we are born—should be a focus and a priority. A lot of times it's not. The type of self-examination and reflection required to learn these behaviors is important for people of all ages and can lead to very positive results.

Education plays a very important role in the lives of people who give a darn. Although educational attainment in the United States between the 2000 and 2017 generally rose, there is a much greater need to focus on character education in our schools. It is just not happening adequately. It is the best way to reach a majority of people since most children attend school for at least some portion of their childhood.

Here is the problem: When it comes to providing social and moral education outside the traditional classroom, it is basically non-existent. And I am not only talking about the home environment, either. In the past, most of the character education we received occurred in our homes and, to a lesser degree, in schools.

With the rise in the number of single-parent families or two-parent families with both parents working outside the home, parents are no longer spending as much time with their children as they did in the past. Unfortunately, the pressures of making a living often means both parents have to work long hours. Children now spend less time at home interacting with their parents or guardians.

As a result, parents are sometimes too busy or distracted to monitor their children's activities. This lack of personal attention has taken a toll. However, if parents cannot always be present, the least they can do is instill the right values in their children's minds. That way, even if their parents are not around, the child knows and does the right thing. If they don't, the child will suffer the consequence of their parents' negligence later on. Modeling desired behaviors is the most effective way to make a lasting impression. If parents are not around their children enough to model Give a Darn behaviors, children are not likely to emulate them.

Children spend eight hours or more at school, followed by some sort of after-school program or activity while their parents are working. By the time children are home with their families, there is little time left for dinner, homework, and the bedtime routine. That leaves even less time for discussions on principles like manners, personal responsibility, accountability, and compassion for others.

In families where children are able to come home right after school, much of their free time is spent watching television or playing video games. High-quality TV shows and games that teach morals and positive values are next to impossible to find. It is a sad day when the one of the most popular video game series among pre-adolescent males is "Grand Theft Auto," where players take on personas as big-city criminals who rise through the ranks of the criminal underworld by completing missions that include assassinations and other violent crimes.

Both formal and character education are the key to really changing society's overall behavior, including preventing crime and other major social ills. There is evidence to support this, and I'll get into it later in this chapter.

Our children learn academic subjects, such as math, science, and history, but we don't often see specific, semester-long courses that teach manners, morals, responsibility, etiquette, character, and how to really give a darn. There are some schools, both public and private, that attempt to provide character education in the classroom. However, the message does not always seem to get across adequately. It's not being taught early enough when children begin to form habits and it is not emphasized enough overall. Further, it is not enough to tell children how they should treat others; adults also need to model these behaviors and set the example.

The best way to change a person's thought process is through direct instruction and modeling. To do this effectively, we have to start at a very early age. My suggestion is to make it a mandatory part of the curriculum as soon as a child begins elementary school. Just like teachers provide classroom lessons each day in math or reading, teachers should also plan for and provide structured lessons on common sense ideas that can be used in everyday life, such as proper and effective communication skills, ways to provide a helping hand, the importance of good manners, how to show gratitude, and much more. Middle school and high school students should take semester- or year-long courses for credit on the subject.

I am quite sure that many schools claim to emphasize these values, but this emphasis usually amounts to little more than motivational posters hung up on classroom walls and then ignored in practice. Give a Darn skills may be underemphasized because social-emotional skills are more difficult to measure than traditional cognitive gains. It might be difficult to capture Give a Darn progress on a test score. But it can be done and, more importantly, it should be done.

Adding these principles to classroom lesson plans and developing courses devoted to them would teach children how to truly incorporate this philosophy into their lives. But the teachers need to be modeling Give a Darn principles as well. The same goes for all other adults in school settings—coaches, cafeteria cooks, principals, custodians, and counselors alike.

There are programs that sponsor special one-time projects or experiences for middle and high school students that promote a Give a Darn attitude towards others. However, these are optional and short-term opportunities. Having a student participate in one or even a handful of such experiences isn't likely to have the same impact as consistent curriculum in character education. It would be ideal if every older child participated each year in at least one service-oriented course and if service-oriented learning could be integrated into classrooms at every elementary grade. I cannot emphasize this enough: It must start at a very early age.

A primary component of this curriculum should be cultivating a positive outlook and a commitment to positive change. Although we can never be perfect, how we frame our imperfections in our minds is what shapes our feelings about them. Think about it. Different ways of framing a situation can either discourage us from continuing or encourage us to persist and do better. It all depends on whether our thinking is positive or negative.

Here is an anecdote about two young golfers to illustrate this point. The first teenager began playing golf and became passionate about the game. He practiced every day, and he got better and better. The aim of golf is to get the ball in the hole with the fewest strokes possible, so most beginner adults shoot over 100. He started shooting in the 90s, then the mid 80s, and then the low 80s. Then, one day, he shot a 75. Par (the number of strokes it should take to complete a game) is around 72 for most 18-hole golf courses, so this was a great score for a young amateur!

But instead of seeing that he was getting better and better and that he had just gotten his best score ever, he got down on himself for his mistakes along the way. He complained that he was only one under par after 12 holes, and then that he had several bogeys (one over par) in a row that ruined his score. When this game was done, he wound up with a 78, just three strokes over par for the course, and he was upset. Instead of building on this accomplishment, he dwelt on a few bad holes.

Meanwhile, a second teen newbie golfer kept getting 7s and 8s on holes (most holes are 3-, 4-, or 5-par) but then got a couple of pars and shot a 105. His thought was, "Wow, I had two great pars on the back nine holes and that is something that I can build on the next time I play."

It is good to keep striving to be the best you can be but not at the expense of negative thinking. A different mindset can change our perception of our abilities, environment, and deeds, as well as how we react to them.

Since people are very impressionable at an early age, they can easily be taught how to care about others. And yet, so often they aren't. Next time you see a 3-, 4- or 5-year-old, think about what is being taught to them about today's society. Small children learn quickly when spending time with adults who are constantly buried in their smartphones. The message that kids receive is that interpersonal communication is not important, especially when they are trying to get their parents' attention. They learn that whatever they think and feel is not nearly as important as what mom or dad is doing or seeing on their phone. We have to change our thinking in order to change the thinking of our future. The kids are it. We can't just tell them the right things to do, we have to show them!

Early childhood is important, but we need to keep emphasizing Give a Darn throughout middle and high school. Research shows that social-emotional learning, such as teaching moral courage to resist peer pressure—which generally results in people doing stupid or crazy things—has huge benefits for our society.

In 2015, Columbia University's Center for Benefit-Cost Studies of Education found this to be true for a variety of Give a Darn-like interventions. The researchers looked at six programs to combat violence and substance abuse, as well as teaching problem solving and emotional management, to try to assess the economic value of social and emotional learning (SEL).

"The most important empirical finding is that each of the six interventions for improving SEL shows measurable benefits that exceed its costs, often by considerable amounts," the center's report stated. "There is a positive return on investments for all of these educational reforms on social and emotional learning." The average benefit-cost ratio for the six programs examined was about $11 for every dollar spent! This certainly reaffirms our position on why an investment in Give a Darn is so important.

One of the programs, called "Life Skills Training," was a classroom intervention to help at-risk students in middle and high school build skills to resist peer pressure. The cost of the program was $13,000 for 100 students. The Columbia researchers found that the benefit came back at more than twice the cost—$32,000 per 100 students in benefits, including avoided vandalism and substance abuse.

Even at a net loss to the taxpayer, it seems that providing our youth with the skills to lead a Give a Darn life would be truly worth the investment. But this study shows that it's well worth the investment in economic terms as well. In other words, a no-brainer.

Higher Education

Randy Pausch rose from working class roots to a legacy as a pioneer in the development of virtual reality. He co-founded Carnegie Mellon University's Entertainment Technology Center and, as a professor of computer science, human-computer interaction, and design, he revolutionized education in computer programming. But he's most widely known for the joyful insights he delivered during his famous final lecture, given roughly a year before he lost his battle to pancreatic cancer.

The "hideous disease," as Randy described it, put his body and family through a toil that many of us can't even imagine. To be one of the only 4 percent who enjoy a five-year survival rate, he underwent extremely invasive surgery, as well as months of brutal chemotherapy and radiation.

His efforts seemed to pay off. He fought the cancer and beat it. But then, it came back. This time it had spread to his liver and spleen. His doctors estimated that he had six months of healthy living ahead of him at most.

What gave him the strength, just one month later, to give his inspiring lecture? He talked about how important it was to show gratitude toward others by saying "thank you" and "please," to find the good in everyone even if it takes years, to work and play well with others, and to always maintain a smile and a positive mood.

"It's not about how to achieve your dreams. It's about how to lead your life," Pausch said. "If you lead your life the right way, the karma will take care of itself. The dreams will come to you."

What hit me the most was how he emphasized the importance of people over things, particularly one person's accountability to others. He said there are three things people should always do if they make a mistake:

1. Say I'm sorry (compassion);

2. Admit that it was your fault (take responsibility for what you do); and

3. Ask the question, "How do I make it right?" (take responsibility for fixing the mistake, no matter how painful it is).

Too many people are graduating from college without learning Randy's message of accountability, positivity, and a regard for other people. College is a great place to educate yourself morally in addition to pursuing your scholarly goals.

For those entering college, please take this grand opportunity to always do the right thing. On the whole, students and young people generally always know what is right and what is wrong. The reason they might do the wrong thing is because they can justify it in their mind as being right. Students and young people should not succumb to this thinking. Why? Because at the end of the day, the truth always comes out. Always.

Of course, everyone makes mistakes. My advice to college kids is to learn now to never give excuses for the mistakes you make. You may have a legitimate one, but it won't benefit you or anyone else to offer it up. Instead, just apologize, accept the consequences, and recommit yourself to a better performance in the future.

People rarely admit when they make a mistake, often choosing to justify it as the fault of some outside force that influences their actions. If things don't go our way, it is not our fault but the fault of someone else, or some circumstance, or the environment. The list is infinite! We are experts at blaming everyone and anything, but not ourselves. People just don't like to admit when they are wrong, although more often than not, they are. We always have an excuse but rarely take responsibility.

Nobody is perfect, but as the saying goes, "It's better to aim at perfection and miss, than to aim at imperfection and hit it." You are going to make mistakes. So, if you make a mistake, admit it, apologize, and then take responsibility to fix it. People really don't expect you to be perfect, but most expect you to be honest (you would think, right?).

I'll conclude my comments on college students with an anecdote about valuing others. A university professor once gave a pop quiz. All of the questions were right from the textbook and lectures until the last question: "What is the first name of the janitor who cleans this building?"

Surely this was a joke, right? Everyone had seen the old man, but how would they know his name? One of the students handed in his quiz, leaving the last question blank. When the class ended, he asked if the last question would count toward the quiz grade.

"Absolutely," the professor said. "In your careers, you will meet many people. All are significant. They deserve your attention and care, even if all you do is smile and say hello." The lesson here

71

is that Give a Darn people value other people, no matter who they are.

What's the key element for student success? In three words, "Give a darn."

Of course, these three words are not traditional, but when you think about it, they certainly drive home a point. Sometimes, we have that tendency to lose the human perspective that determines success. Success is driven by our unique positive or negative contributions, those things that we do that set us apart from others. And yet students—and for that matter, most people—rarely realize how important attitude is toward success.

Quality is a basic ingredient for generating revenue from a product or service. True success, however, isn't about products or services or revenue. Success is really about the value you add personally to what you produce.

College students go to class every day ready to produce moments of truth. Everything a student does creates a moment of truth, and they can make it either positive or negative. Ideally, this value should govern both our personal and professional life. So how can we do this? What can students do to be remembered and respected by teachers, family, and friends? It's fairly simple—give a darn.

It's a service mantra philosophy of how we can contribute to making our world a better place to live and breathe, and to reduce violence. It is how we should live our life.

I have instilled this attitude in the many student interns that I have hired to help me with my business, driving home the point that being self-centered is not only dangerous, it's a one-way ticket to failure, violence, and bad relationships. Students need to remember that it's not grades, promotions, and raises that get you ahead, it's what you do for others. It was an ah-ha moment for all my interns. Responsible, accountable, and respectful—that's what it means to give a darn.

The adoption of the Give a Darn philosophy is truly a student's path to success.

Chapter 5 – Give a Damn on Teams

I get tired of professional athletes making zillions of dollars and then, after having a good season, complaining that they deserve more. They want their multiyear contract re-negotiated. It's just wrong. What happens if they have a bad season? Do they go to management and say, "I want to re-negotiate my contract to a lower salary because I did not do very well last season?" Of course not.

And have you ever heard management ask a player to take a lesser salary in the middle of a contract because they played badly the previous year? A player makes a commitment to a contract because he feels that, at the time, it is fair or a good deal. If we agree to something, we should honor that commitment regardless of the circumstances that might come later. Setbacks and unexpected successes happen, but they should never lead to dishonoring a commitment.

This brings up a great example of a player in my own backyard for whom I have a lot of respect. The New Orleans Saints' Drew Brees is probably one of the best NFL quarterbacks to ever play the game. But my admiration for him is much greater due to his conduct off the field.

In 2006, Brees signed a six-year, $60 million contract with the Saints, which had one of the most potent offenses in the NFL during his contract term. Brees set numerous records and the Saints even won the Superbowl in 2010. But did he ever demand a re-negotiation of his contract because he did so well? Not a chance. So many others have done it in practically all team sports. An athlete has a great year and he wants to renegotiate his contract because now he feels he did not get a fair deal. He even threatens to sit out a year until he gets what he wants. Very sad.

NFL contract negotiations are notoriously intense, with high stakes for the players, teams, lawyers, agents, and fans. The process is complex, with lots of stats involved, as well as considerations for timing constraints, salary caps, contract lengths, and player issues like aging and injury. But that should not take away from doing what is right.

When Brees' contract ran out in 2011, he stated that he would be "beyond stunned" if he and the Saints were unable to agree on a contract extension, echoing comments made by coach Sean Payton. Brees said that he did not believe his next deal would prevent the Saints from bidding on other key members of their record-setting offense who were to become free agents.

"My No. 1 priority, and it always has been this, is keeping our team together and making sure we have the right guys in the right positions to make a run at this for a long time," Brees told the Associated Press. "We all kind of work together on this thing. Put it this way: I'm not worried one bit about my contract or our ability to keep guys at key positions." In the end, Brees and the Saints reached a five-year, $100 million deal that balanced short-term flexibility for the Saints with a salary that reflected Brees' value to the team. He became one of the highest-paid quarterbacks in the NFL.

For the next five years, Brees continued to set NFL records, and he 100 percent honored his agreement with the team. In 2018, a new round of negotiations ensured that Brees would stay with the Saints for two more years for $50 million. The deal was seen by some as Brees taking less than market value to stay in his beloved New Orleans, where he is invested in business and philanthropic pursuits. In my view, he agreed to a balance between what is right for his family, what is right for the team, and what is right for the city.

Brees is absolutely what this book is all about. He is an upstanding individual who truly gives a damn and is one of the most respected and admired players in the NFL. If more people adopted an attitude like Brees, this world would be a much better place. Thank you, Drew Brees, for setting this positive example for the world to hopefully model one day.

Give a Damn people put the goals of the team before their own. We all have individual goals. But when you sacrifice a team goal for an individual goal, you are thinking like a self-centered person.

Let me bring up another example concerning the New Orleans Saints. In December 2017, the Saints were battling their chief rival, the Atlanta Falcons, in a hotly contested game on Atlanta's home turf. The Falcons' star running back, Devonta Freeman, was giving all he could, despite having suffered concussions during the year, to help the team win one of the final games of the season.

In the fourth quarter of this highly competitive game, Freeman was stopped for no gain near the Saints' sideline. In the heat of the moment, Payton mocked him with a gesture that looked like choking. The gesture was a reference to the Falcons losing the Super Bowl earlier that year after having had a 28–3 lead over the New England Patriots. The Saints ultimately lost that day in Atlanta. In comments to the press reflecting on the game, Payton expressed sincere and humble regret about his inappropriate action.

"Listen, the mistake I made that night was letting my emotions get the best of me," he said. "It's the same thing that we talk about with our players all of the time. It wasn't good, and I felt like as that game went on, it even affected me in calling plays. I've got to (do) better that way."

There are a few strong lessons here for everyone to learn regarding Payton's action and his response afterwards. The Saints learned that character is a huge and important element in putting a team together, and I think they model that from the top down.

Team Character

Teamwork revolves around character. It involves thinking about others first and what is good for the team. It involves motivating people even if you are not the star player or first or second string. Character is the difference maker when it comes to championship teams.

To give a damn, character means working with an attitude of altruism. It means honoring your commitments, putting in more than you're getting paid for, doing tasks that aren't covered by the scope of your job description, practicing positivity in negative situations, working hard toward team goals, and celebrating success. Everyone on a team that gives a damn becomes a champion.

Unfortunately, people just don't always understand or truly believe in this philosophy. These team-oriented character traits are all too rare in the workplace. There are too many people with a 9-to-5 mindset. It doesn't matter what needs to be done; they leave at 5 p.m. sharp. They only have jobs because jobs pay them money.

Let's say you are at work and have a really important project to get out. It's 3 p.m. and you have two hours to get it done in order to meet a deadline and you cannot get it done alone. You know you need help, so you ask your associate (let's call him Pete) to make copies so you can meet your fast-approaching deadline. Upon hearing your request, Pete replies, "Sorry, that's just not my job."

You think, "Really?" and then you are quick to add, "Pete, I really need to get this done. I will give you 50 bucks if you help me." Without hesitation, Pete says, "Sure!"

Now Pete offers his help because it has a material benefit for him, which took precedence over helping you. There seems to be a growing trend that people are less likely to do good things for others simply because it is the right thing to do. Rather, they need some kind of reward, like money, or accolade to motivate them. It is a sad and disturbing tendency that is becoming more prevalent every day.

When people do their jobs without truly caring about the effort they put into it, they only do what they are supposed to do. No more than that and, if possible, less. Sadly, in today's society, the mere mention of effort is taboo. And yet we want to be rewarded greatly for participating with little to no effort.

All it takes is one individual to outwardly act in a self-centered way for it to have a cancerous effect on the team. The problem with many teams who might have great talent is that they think individually and therefore never become a real team or live up to expectations.

People should take a job to make a difference; the money is just icing on the cake. People need to take pride in their work, which seems to be increasingly rare. Sometimes we encounter a person who says, "I love my job *and* I get paid for doing it!" They find it unbelievable that they are getting paid for something that they love to do.

Of course, we can't all land a job that seems purposeful and enjoyable on a daily basis. But there's good news! Even if you are in job that you truly don't like, if you practice the Give a Damn attitude, you will like it better. The more we care about something, the more interesting it becomes.

Some do this well; others do not. One phrase that I truly abhor is, "That's not my job." You work for a company and respond to a request for help by saying, "That's not my job?" This is the ultimate message that reveals to me who you really are and how you think. This is what a self-centered person would say. They don't give a damn about helping anyone unless it serves their best interest. If they can personally benefit, then they will help. The reason why some serve others poorly is that they don't give a damn; they work only because they must to survive.

In the summer of 2016, a road crew was repainting the yellow stripes running down the center of Route 460, which passes through Prince George County, Va. On a stretch near the James River, the crew encountered a dead raccoon. Supposedly, because it was not the job of the street painters to remove the dead animal in the middle of the road before painting it, they simply painted over it. Locals were shocked to find a dead animal in the road covered with a yellow stripe.

You can only shake your head at this one. This is a classic example of a "That's not my job!" attitude.

People with this kind of attitude are generally unhappy because they only think about serving themselves and their basic needs. They fail to realize that one has to go beyond meeting his or her material needs in order to truly thrive and achieve greater success.

This type of attitude is becoming far too pervasive in our society. Many people expect the best, but they are only willing to put in a minimum of effort to get it. Some may call this efficiency, but there is a difference between efficiency and laziness!

I recently came across a sign outside a New Orleans business that read, "Are you proud of your work today?" It really makes you think.

If you're like most, chances are you've had to work with a person with a bad attitude—someone who is not committed to their work, their customers, or other team members. They're toxic and a drain on you and everybody else around them. It's not exactly fun working with someone who takes no pride in their job. They bring people down.

On the other hand, you've also likely worked with people who have positive energy and radiate this to everyone around them. Those with a positive attitude not only help get things done, but they make the workplace more satisfying for others. They create a synergy that enhances the entire team. They bring people up.

But here is the sad part: A-level players don't want to be around C-level players. In fact, the best way for a company to lose its top employees is to allow its workplace culture to foster negativity, bad attitudes, and a lack of pride and commitment.

Whenever someone asks me how I am, I always respond with a boisterous, "Terrific!" Every time I say this I generally shock people, but I always get a smile, as if I am crazy. Of course, I am not always terrific, but this response lightens the attitudes of those around me. One of my employees asked one day, "How can you be terrific every day?" I told her with a smile on my face, "It's because some days are just more terrific than others."

One of the many things Give a Damn people seem to have in common is an appreciation for achievement—their own and, more importantly, that of others. They focus on the team being successful, because then everybody wins. They understand that accomplishments are one of the best ways to motivate people, including themselves and their coworkers. Success is something to be enjoyed, celebrated, and encouraged. Give a Damn people are cheerleaders for positive contributions.

Everyone wants to work with people like this. Give a Damn employees do things cooperatively, enthusiastically, and with a minimum of problems. You need that from others and they need it from you. So, what are you doing to make that happen? Are you a contributor or are you getting in the way? What, exactly, are you doing to build commitment and positive attitudes?

Give a Damn people know how to collaborate because behaviors like altruism, hard work, positivity, commitment, and kindness make the collective success of a team, department, or company possible. Collaborative people can be team members, colleagues, helpers, partners, co-workers, compatriots, and more. There is never an occasion on which they ask themselves, "What's in it for me?" because that's not their primary goal.

If you care about the people you work with then you care about how your actions impact them. That makes you more likely to take steps to help them work effectively and less likely to put off a response they need. The "What's in it for me?" attitude is not associated with giving a damn, because Give a Damn people know something good will come out of it in the end. You win when everyone else wins.

In Chapter 10, I'll discuss practical steps for cultivating the Give a Damn attitude on an individual and group basis. Boosting your commitment and attitude, as well as that of others, is a challenge that requires you to invest time, attention, and effort. But it's worth the investment. Everyone will reap the benefits of an engaging work environment that produces more rewards for all, including you. It brings everyone up!

Team Benefits

At 13 years old, I took over the morning newspaper delivery route for the *Democrat & Chronicle* in Rochester, N.Y. Paper delivery requires you to get up really early in the morning but is otherwise a relatively simple job. However, my route had one big wrinkle: When I took it over, all 61 of my customers were pretty upset for a host of reasons.

The paper was rarely delivered before people headed to work—and sometimes never arrived. On rainy days, the waterlogged papers were unreadable. After hearing about all the issues and complaints, I understood their needs and was motivated to do things differently.

I knew that customers wanted to read the paper before they went to work. So, I began getting up at about 5 a.m., got my bundle of newspapers, and made sure that all the papers were delivered no later than 6:30 each morning. I decided that people did not need to go outside to get their paper so I put it in between each customer's screen and front doors. This made a huge difference on rainy days and throughout the winter.

I wanted to do things differently and go beyond my customers' expectations. It became really rewarding to me because people were very appreciative of what I was doing. Their simple thankfulness was very gratifying for me. In 1971, after my first full year as a paper boy, I'm proud to say that I was awarded "Newspaper Boy of the Year" by the Gannett Company. I continued on the job for four years. Several years later, when I graduated from high school, Gannett awarded me a scholarship to Boston College for my efforts.

Being part of the *Democrat & Chronicle* team for several years paid off in multiple ways. Not only did I get paid for the hours worked, but I also received recognition for going above and beyond what people expected. And I received financial support for my education. But most of all, the experience taught me basic skills in making customers happy and what is needed for entrepreneurial success. The lessons and guidance that I received from so many people paid off multiple times in college and in my career, and I'm so grateful to have learned them at such an early age. I was truly blessed.

In every job, you work for money. But you must also serve others in some capacity, which, in effect, serves you. Whether you work for a company, a government agency, or a nonprofit, your actions should be performed as a service to that institution and in alignment with its goals. If we went into a work situation with the total desire to help others, I believe that our food and shelter would naturally be provided.

Most people either don't understand or don't trust this statement. Therefore, they provide excuses for why something cannot be done or for why they might feel entitled to receive something. During Hurricane Katrina recovery under the Nagin administration, New Orleans employees who had city credit cards racked up exorbitant charges for travel, hotels, and fine meals. These cards were the financial responsibility of the city. Although one would expect the city to cover reasonable meal expenses for business or lobbying meetings, one charge was for over $3,800 at a steakhouse.

The administration said the bill covered a dinner hosted by Nagin's executive staff for city council members and the city's legislators, including space for the staff to make an audio-visual presentation. But it appears to me that this bill—and others detailed in the news—was still excessively high. It brought to mind this question: Do you think that these employees would have racked up these same kinds of charges if they were paying out of their own pocket? I doubt it.

Your mindset is usually different when you are paying with someone else's (like your company's) money. When it doesn't affect you, your Give a Damn barometer goes way down. Why? Because your mindset might shift to one of entitlement, causing you to think something along the lines of, "The city can afford it, and I deserve it because of all the hard work I do."

But what if you had to foot the entire bill yourself? Would your thinking change? Of course it would! We should all spend other people's money like it's our own, even if that person or organization is wealthy.

But it doesn't just come down to obvious moral conflicts like the improper use of your employer's credit card. The same moral concerns should come into play when you're thinking about moving on from an organization that helped you grow professionally.

Employee turnover is very expensive for any organization. Research shows that it can cost more than 200 percent of your annual salary for your employer to recruit, choose, and train your replacement. And that doesn't even take into consideration the other costs your employer faces, like the loss of your institutional knowledge and the social networks you built while working there.

There are often very good reasons for an employee to leave a work situation, but other times, the motivation is a marginal pay increase or title improvement. People should be more concerned about what they can put into a situation than what they can get out of it. Too many people get it reversed by thinking, "What's in it for me?"

Give a Damn thinking isn't like that. You think about others and what is best for them, not for yourself. What people don't realize is that, in almost every case, you will get something out of it. But you should never expect it.

In most instances you will (or should) at least get a simple thank you. This simple gesture should provide you with the satisfaction that you helped someone. But I believe that, if you work for an organization that gives a damn, you'll get much more.

My stint as a paper boy wasn't the end of my good luck with business institutions. I have gained many material and non-material benefits by having a long-term relationship with my employers.

IBM is another good example. I always saw myself as an entrepreneur, so when I first joined the company, I thought I'd be there maybe three years at the most. But I found success at IBM and they treated me well. So, I stayed, grew, and learned from them for more than 13 years.

During that time, I benefited tremendously from being part of a large company that was respected for quality and service. Being surrounded by the excellent talent that the company attracted pushed me to be more successful in my own life. Through my daily interactions with coworkers, I learned about the qualities that made them successful, and I developed close personal friendships. IBM had great incentives with highly motivating material and non-material rewards. This is also, by the way, the job that kept me in New Orleans after graduating from Tulane University, and for that I'll be forever grateful.

Maybe it sounds too good to be true that you will get something out of your service and commitment to the institution that employs you. However, I can assure you that, from my own experiences and from the many Give a Damn people that I have talked to, it is a fact.

Plus, it doesn't cost any money, at least up front, to test this theory for yourself. You won't lose anything by trying out my Give a Damn philosophy, and you could have everything to gain. But if you do something wrong, you will eventually have to pay for it monetarily or otherwise, because the truth always wins.

Of course, if you work in a corrupt or toxic environment, or you're a member of a team that rewards short-term gains or disrespectful behavior, applying Give a Damn behaviors may cost you in a material sense, at least in the short term. But moral courage is a fundamental aspect of Give a Damn. You should never feel ashamed or afraid of doing what is right, especially if it's to the benefit of others.

It's no simple task, I know. And I have asked this question before: Would you change the things you say or do if you knew that someone (your mom, for example) was watching every move you made? Would you give a damn more than you do now? I am sure that you would because most of us don't want to disappoint our mom. So, a good way to get in the habit of giving a damn is to pretend that there is someone watching you all the time, someone you would never want to disappoint. Every time you approach a task, look at it as if you are doing the job for yourself, a loved one, or your family. When you do this, you will always focus on doing the best job possible.

This means thinking ahead and not just concentrating on the now. Doing your best work will benefit you and others in the long term.

If you work for an institution that has clear goals for growth and success, values adherence to the law, and celebrates employees who conduct themselves with courtesy, professionalism, and positivity, then it's much easier to give a damn at work. Here's all you have to do: Work with an attitude of love and excellence, be mindful of the long-term impact of your work, and react with a calm and open mind to conflict and criticism.

Finally, even in a Give a Damn workplace, interactions aren't always pleasant. It is important to allow others to share their ideas with you, even if their ideas conflict with yours. Before getting defensive about seemingly critical comments—especially if they are directed at you—pause to listen and consider. Often, when people say something to or about us that is perceived to be critical we immediately become defensive. We think about what the person has said and how it was said, but we don't always think about the reason for the comment.

In many situations, criticism from others can be constructive if we remain open to it. Criticism from others should be viewed as an opportunity for self-improvement. In most situations, there is some element of truth in what has been said, even if delivered in a bad way. We just don't want to admit it. If you listen intently to *what* is being said and not the way it is being said—which can put you on the defensive—you might be able to find something to improve upon.

On the flip side, unless you are someone's manager, it is best to offer constructive criticism to others *only* when your feedback has been solicited. And then, the key is to offer comments in a way that shows you give a damn about the other person. One of the reasons I worked for IBM is that they provided great training for their employees. I knew that this professional development would benefit me in launching my entrepreneurial career if I ever were to leave. But it was tough at times.

I started in an office products sales position, focusing on typewriters and copiers. To learn all the features and benefits of the products, IBM immediately sent me and about 10 other new hires to Dallas for three weeks of intense training. One of the biggest challenges was a trainer who gave me the worst kind of tough love.

He criticized me all the time. Everything I did was wrong, wrong, wrong. It got really frustrating for me because it felt like I was continually being beaten up and had never been told what I was doing right. I finally said something to the trainer and asked if he could please tell me one thing I was doing right so that I could build upon it. He did, and I got better and better. At the end of the day, I completed the training and the experience worked out to my benefit.

Being on the receiving end of criticism made me realize that we don't compliment people often enough when something is done well. I wasn't getting any praise to balance out the tough love. Compliments lift people up and make them happy, motivating them to do better. Even if you know some people who have a hard time accepting compliments, it is still the right thing to do. To quote the old milk ad campaign, "It does a body good." And receiving all that criticism during corporate training helped me internalize this lesson in a meaningful way.

Another example of the benefits of criticism comes from outside the workplace, but it applies here as well. Several cities have installed red light cameras at busy intersections to catch people running red lights or speeding. If someone runs a red light, a picture of the license plate is taken and a ticket is mailed to their home.

What's wrong with this? Nothing. In fact, it is also an opportunity to make people more aware of their driving habits. This is exactly what it did for me. I got a camera speeding ticket for going 45 in a 30 mph zone, and since then I've been much more conscientious about maintaining driving habits that contribute to the safety of my community. So what if people think it is a money grab for local government? If you don't speed or run a red light, then you have nothing to worry about. By not having these cameras, does it give you the right or opportunity to speed and therefore not get caught? These cameras encourage safe driving, so I consider them a good thing.

Before I close my comments on the value of service to a team or organization, I want to bring up another example from my beloved New Orleans Saints. For two seasons, former Saints running back Deuce McAllister suffered from torn ligaments in both knees. He rehabbed his first knee after tearing it in the middle of the season, returned, and tore the ligament in his other knee, sending him back through the same rigorous treatment.

Before the second knee was rehabbed, McAllister was supposed to get a $1 million roster signing bonus. He could have demanded this signing bonus even though he still had not fully recovered from his second knee injury; instead, he agreed to defer the bonus until such time that he could see if he could play again. Because of his selflessness, the team saved more than $4 million in salary-cap space.

He could have demanded the bonus but didn't. Why would he behave in this way? Because he is not a greedy or self-centered person. How many times have you ever heard of such an act in pro sports? Probably never. He thought about the team and their interest before he thought of himself. I so admire that about McAllister. Like Brees, he is a quality individual.

When McAllister and the Saints parted ways in 2009, Executive Vice President and General Manager Mickey Loomis told the press, "Deuce has epitomized hard work, leadership and productivity throughout his career and has been a source of great pride for all of us associated with the team." Still a fan favorite, McAllister became the WWL Radio color commentator for Saints' football games in 2016 and was hired in 2018 as the Saints' play-by-play analyst for the New Orleans Fox affiliate WVUE.

The team approach always boils down to quality and concern for others. Or, in other words, give a damn in everything you do for your employer. It will benefit you, your department, and your colleagues.

Chapter 6 – Give a Damn in Management

ABB is a global and pioneering technology company that is more than a century old. They work in a number of industries that provide cutting-edge services like digital transformation. The company's UK Power Systems Division builds substations, renewable energy converter stations, and other multi-million dollar energy construction projects. They have a long history of success but, like every other company, they have also had challenges, such as supply chain delays and other impediments to project flow.

As with any good company that needs to implement cultural change, ABB started by setting clear and strategic goals for the division. They wanted to, among other things, improve employee engagement and increase revenue. But to achieve their goals, they took an unorthodox approach to improving leadership.

Rather than micromanage their managers' behavior, the approach focused on broad principles, such as responsibility and respect. The division evaluated managers on the extent to which they currently lived the principles. Next, they engaged and equipped them with helpful content on best practices and then embedded them in small groups. The latter worked by leveraging peer pressure for continued improvement. Like the Give a Damn movement, ABB's initiative shows how herd mentality can be used to achieve good results.

The principle-based program transformed UK Power Systems into a highly successful division. Due to its success, ABB implemented this culture change initiative across additional business areas. This program, which focused on responsibility and respect, led to the company expanding into new markets and significantly growing their business. Not only did this principles-first approach raise revenue, as outlined in a case study in *Training Journal* magazine, but morality and teamwork within the division was greatly boosted.

JavaPresse Coffee Company is an e-commerce startup that uses their virtual workforce to deliver high-end coffee and brewing gear to coffee aficionados throughout the world. Its founder, Raj

Jana, launched the company after the death of a beloved mentor prompted him to rethink his corporate goals.

Jana had a passion for the meaning and fulfillment he associated with the pleasures of drinking good coffee, and he wanted to bring that good feeling to other people. But as anyone who's run a startup knows, the daily grind of growing a company from scratch can easily suck the passion out of even the most passionate people.

But Jana had a secret strategy, and he used it to grow his company 800 percent in just one year. The strategy was so simple that you scratch your head when you hear it. But he's more than happy to share his secret: gratitude.

"Gratitude is a practice that helps you feel good about who you are, what you have and what you're doing," Jana wrote in *Entrepreneur* magazine. "It helps you connect more deeply with yourself and others while empowering a heightened sense of purpose. Combining this concept with strategic goal-setting transforms it into a business game changer."

From well-established global infrastructure companies to boutique startups, the message is the same. Give a Damn leadership is essential. Leadership on Give a Damn principles can solve major organizational challenges, raise revenue, and help retain valuable employees. But more importantly, it can ensure that your company has a positive impact on the world.

My first experience with a major turnaround came when I first took over the Louisiana Technology Council in late 2002, the same year Nagin was elected. I had sold my internet services startup, gone into consulting, and accepted a position on the LTC board.

The LTC was in bad shape. It was heavily in debt, membership was declining, and the members we had retained were just not happy with the benefits the organization was providing. In fact, the LTC was almost on the brink of collapse.

In all this chaos, I saw an opportunity. I could expand my skillset as a consultant through hands-on learning by turning around an organization that was in really bad shape. At the same time, I could also play a long-term role in elevating Louisiana's reputation and capacity for technology work, which was basically non-existent. So, I took the job.

During the first month, I was not paid because we simply did not have the money. One of my objectives was to establish a brand or a theme that everyone could rally around, so I created and copyrighted the slogan: "Louisiana: Tech Capital of the South." At the time, Louisiana was almost dead last in technology employment. Everyone thought I was crazy. In 2002, the thought of the words "Louisiana" and "technology" together was absurd.

I put together a plan, presented it to the membership, and told them that if we could not turn the LTC around within a year we would shut it down and move on. Well, we didn't have to. In fact, I went on to run the council for more than 10 years. During that time, Louisiana's technology employment went from 49th (2007) to 32nd (2010).

As you already know, the job would also give me the opportunity to test my resolve as an empowered citizen and member of the New Orleans technology community by speaking out about corruption in the Nagin administration. But I'll get back to that story again a bit later.

In this chapter, we'll look at leadership through the lens of three critical aspects of a successful company: the culture its employees work in, the safety of the environment it operates in, and the respect that is (or should be) pervasive at all levels.

Culture

Many people today are unhappy with their jobs. Much of this has to do with culture. And the good news is that culture is something that leadership can transform in a concrete and constructive way.

Corporate culture is the unseen and emotional system in which you operate at work. It is the collective norms, expectations, and assumptions inside a business. Culture has a big effect on how employees think and act. And employee actions have a huge impact on how well a company responds to the challenges that it will face. That makes dealing with company culture hugely important.

In my business consulting work, I often advise clients on employee recruitment and retention. That's where culture starts— getting the right people with the right mindset and in the right position. My hiring philosophy is that when you interview a new candidate, their experience isn't nearly the most important thing. Of course, their resume must show that they can fulfill your company's job requirements, but at the end of the day you should focus critically on how a candidate would fit into the culture of the organization.

As a result, I've developed a unique interview guide that encourages my clients to get away from the typical Q&A interview format. My guide focuses instead on prompts. For instance, I want to know the first thing that comes to a job candidate's mind when I give them prompts like favorite color, favorite movie, five single words that best describe them, and more. There are more than 70 prompts on my list.

The whole idea is to shift your focus away from what a candidate is capable of doing and toward how they think. This gives you a much better understanding of how they would fit into your business' culture. It's unconventional, and no one can prepare for such an interview. That's part of why it works.

If you're trying to turn around a negative culture in a workforce that's already fully developed, the challenge is, of course, much harder. You don't want to fire people en masse. Starting from scratch with new employees wouldn't help much either, since you're bringing them into a business with a broken culture.

So, start with strategic and measurable goals. They could include improving customer service, increasing sales, or achieving any other metric of success. Then, create a plan to bring your employees along for the ride.

It often makes sense to start with management because they feed into the rest of the company's culture. People need to feel part of a team, and it starts at the top. You must make cultural changes among management to elevate their leadership. Often this requires changing management's outlook so that they can see exactly how the work that they're doing for the organization is succeeding—and, by the way, rewarding them for it. But if it means replacing people, so be it.

It's not enough to be a manager—you must be a true leader. So, what's the difference between the two? A successful manager is a leader, but there are subtle differences.

Both need the ability to build relationships and provide the right incentives and motivation that drive people to want to succeed. It is not an easy thing to do because every person has different motivational buttons. A true leader understands and rewards employee contributions so that momentum and success continue forward.

The most important distinction is that leaders have people that want to follow them, while managers have people who want to work for them. Both managers and leaders are important. Both have to engage personnel in turning a company's vision into reality, but it's the leader that creates the culture that drives it. Leaders paint a picture of what they see as possible, get feedback and buy in from everyone, and then inspire their people to turn vision into reality. People want to follow them because it feels inspiring.

Leaders do not like the status quo. They are disrupters and innovators. And the good ones do it in everyone's best interest while aligned with what is best for the company. They like change and, even though a company might be achieving great success, they know there might be a better way.

A manager must meet short-term goals and objectives. But a leader strives to go beyond their capabilities and help others to do the same. Leaders want to continue to grow personally, acquiring new knowledge that can enhance the success of the company and their employees. They feel that if they are not learning something every day they might fall behind. Perfecting the skills that got them to where they are just isn't enough.

Successful leaders rely on their vision to motivate, influence, and provide the resources needed to help other managers and employees grow and realize the organization's vision. Leaders build loyalty, trust, and respect by consistently delivering on their promise and doing the right thing. Successful leaders know how to give a damn.

Successful leaders change culture by implementing motivational and developmental programs that raise employee culture to the desired level of excellence. Leaders must engage all employees at a level where they feel like they're part of something that can be successful. People must feel empowered to make a difference. Otherwise they're just doing their job, and you've got a workforce full of 9-to-5 people who don't give a damn.

Leaders give employees the power to contribute to something that they can get satisfaction from. They empower people to take reasonable and calculated risks and chances. Empowerment works if you reward those you empower in some meaningful way. You can use peer recognition, bonuses, or even paid days off as a reward for employees modeling the principles of your newly elevated culture of giving a damn.

Safety

Companies often think that safety comes down to having perfectly written policies and procedures—and enforcing them with a hard line. A major issue with a lot of people today is that they feel they must control everything. Control means you have to win, no matter the cost, to fulfill your interests or boost your ego. But in my experience in the corporate sector, startups, and business consulting, empowering employees to create their own safety and success is a much better way to achieve the goals of the organization.

Managers need to make sure that goals are reached. They must put strategies and procedures into place so that personnel can objectively measure their contributions toward company success. But it's critical that employees feel the sense of accomplishment that only comes from making a difference. The successful leader creates the vision but involves employees in designing the strategies needed to implement that vision.

Managers assign tasks to people and provide detailed guidance on how to accomplish them in order to meet a specific objective. But true leaders know what they don't know. They get the experts to do a particular job and let them do it. They embrace people who know more than they do without feeling threatened. Leaders empower employees to do what they do best and resist the temptation of telling them exactly how to do it. By empowering employees to succeed and understanding that failure is part of the process, people can grow and learn.

What I'm saying may be reminiscent of the Kaizen approach made famous by case studies on Toyota's manufacturing process. Kaizen refers to empowering employees to make small and continuous improvements.

Rather than trying to create perfect processes and expecting perfect compliance from employees, Toyota allows their employees on the manufacturing floor to help design their own processes. It empowers people to think about improving safety. Rather than just avoiding slip-ups while repeating mundane tasks over and over, they pay more attention to their work and how it ties into the bigger picture.

Within the Toyota system, working safely means "understanding good and bad work habits to avoid accidents and professional illnesses." Kaizen reduces the number of errors, but not by prescribing rigid practices. It works by teaching people how to recognize when they're violating a clear standard, so they can self-correct.

Most of us can come up with a list of people who have demonstrated through their actions that they gave a damn and others who did not. The following sign was taken off the inside door of a men's bathroom where I used to work. For months, someone kept throwing paper towels on the floor after drying his hands, despite the fact that the waste basket was only four feet away from the exit door. Eventually, the cleaning lady got fed up and placed a sign on the door that read:

> This is intended for the individual who keeps dropping paper towels on the floor here at the door. I assume you are drying your hands with the towels and in some extreme, fastidious sense of cleanliness, you hope to avoid germs by opening the door using the towel as a shield. Then you simply drop the towel on the floor as you leave. Good move, but a selfish act, since somebody has to come along behind you and pick up your soiled towel. Please, in the future, simply open the door using the towel as you have in the past, but take the towel with you and drop it in the trash can in your office.

Would this person do the same thing in his own house? Probably not! He wouldn't want to risk his family members slipping on or being infected with the germ-ridden towels.

Another example of a self-centered behavior that posed a significant safety risk was when I observed a man washing windows in a building where I worked. He had just washed two windows directly above the glass door going in and out of the building. When the door opened up, I noticed a pool of water on the tile floor. This was a ticket for disaster. People exiting the building might slip.

As I was leaving I had to gingerly walk through the water for fear of slipping myself (there was no way around it, so you had to walk through or hop over it). The washer had no concern about the water on the floor that could cause someone to slip and get hurt. He hadn't even bothered to put up a wet floor sign. The probability of someone slipping and falling was high and, if this had happened, the cleaning company could have been sued.

If this same person was washing windows over the front door and his 85-year-old father came out with the pool of water on the floor, what do you think he would have done? Damn right, he would have made sure the water was gone so his father would not slip and fall. We have to think about how our actions might affect others, no matter who they are.

I asked the window washer if he had a towel that I could wipe the floor with so no one would slip coming in or out of the building. He became a bit flustered and said, "I'll get it," and he immediately cleaned up the water. I was a bit confused and thought that he must have been oblivious to what he was doing or just did not give a damn.

Asking if these unsanitary and unsafe practices would be practiced in your own home is not just a rhetorical question. In the previous chapter, I discussed the thought exercise of asking yourself whether you'd change the things you say or do if you knew that someone like mom was watching every move you made. I also argued that people should be more concerned about what they can put into a work situation than what they can get out of it.

Companies should expect their employees to act with a respectful, accountable, and service-oriented approach. But as the research shows, leaders can be the real drivers of this change by providing employees with a Give a Damn culture.

Take a cue from Kaizen by making culture changes that promote empowerment and safety. Make it clear that everyone is expected to be engaged with the standards that govern their environment and their work. It's the only way to ensure that small problems like messy bathrooms and dripping wet floors won't turn into illness and injury.

And it allows people to creatively improve standards and uplift the company. In short, it engages people to give a damn about their work.

But too many managers dismiss employee contributions to an organization. If an employee brings up a problem, it's important to consider that they may be noticing something that you as a manager may simply not be privy to or know about.

Encourage employees to bring these problems up, and give them credit for valuable contributions. And instead of coming in with your own solution, give them a chance to solve it themselves.

Giving a damn about a safe and healthy workplace starts with management taking a hard look at themselves.

Respect

Some people let power and money go to their heads and think they are above other people. They consider themselves better than those around them, but they often spend their lives in fear of losing even a small portion of their worldly possessions and influence. Their wealth gives them outer strength, but they are often weak and afraid on the inside. I am not sure why, but I suspect it would be for fear of losing it all.

There are many executives who refuse to do tasks that they feel are beneath them out of fear it will affect their status. In fact, it's a matter of their egos getting in the way, not their status. What do you think this says about them? It shows that they are not team players and feel that they are better than others. Who wants to do business with this kind of person?

An unfortunate result of this is that leadership in corporate America typically does not empower enough people to go the extra mile and give a damn. Many organizations don't encourage creativity or individuality to serve others.

People who give a damn do not feel like they are somehow above other people, regardless of education, experience, socioeconomic status, or any other trait. Successful CEOs treat everyone from the vice president to the janitor as someone of importance.

It doesn't matter if you are the head of a major organization or a small retail store. If you give a damn, you will let your esteem for others shine through your words and actions.

Give a Damn people are leaders who want to help others, even if it means putting in the extra work. It's just the right thing to do. If you know how to give a damn, leaders will come to you for help, which now makes you a leader as well!

Simple gestures, such as returning an email, getting a drink for someone, or not keeping a person waiting for an appointment, are important Give a Damn examples of what the president of a corporation of any size should do. This Give a Damn attitude will then translate to other employees, causing the company to become much more successful.

Create something that people just cannot walk away from. Create a work environment attitude that people want to be around. This will then influence and inspire them to become a Give a Damn person just like you. A Give a Damn attitude is contagious!

This viral effect is important because every member of an organization should have the same Give a Damn attitude, whether they are the president or a custodian. Each is just as important as the other. Just having a title does not mean you are entitled to a self-centered attitude.

In fact, as I'll discuss further in the next chapter, professionals who are in customer service positions, rather than management, are some of the most important people in any organization. Customer service professionals who excel at their job are models for the rest of us—not just for their own colleagues and managers, but for everyone navigating the world and interacting with challenging people.

Chapter 7 – Give a Damn in Customer Service

In the spring of 2017, an 8-year-old boy named Noah needed to travel to the Cleveland Clinic for tests and procedures for a heart defect. His doctors determined that he would eventually need a heart transplant. In the meantime, his team of doctors was working to keep him strong.

Noah's grandfather, Clem, called Delta Air Lines for insight on getting the best possible airfare and to book tickets for the family to travel there. Unfortunately, this probably wouldn't be the only occasion for such a trip. During the conversation, Katie Suitter, the Delta customer service representative who spoke with Clem, learned the reason for the trip, as well as the fact that Noah had an upcoming birthday.

Suitter, a mother of three boys herself, had experienced the trauma of her own child having had multiple surgeries and medical appointments. She knew the terrible uncertainty of having to go through an experience like Noah's. Her empathy for Noah and his family drove her to do more than just book the best fare.

Suitter put together a care package especially for Noah. She filled a blue airplane backpack with activity books, colored pencils, an iTunes gift card, and a Delta Cool Your Jets hat. And when the backpack Suitter wanted for Noah was out of stock and unavailable for backorder, she bid on and won it from a company silent auction instead.

In addition to the backpack, Suitter also sent a collapsible travel cooler loaded with snacks and a journal for Noah's mom. And she sent it all out before Noah's birthday.

Don't be ashamed if this story brings tears to your eyes. It's incredibly touching. But this isn't that much of an anomaly for Suitter. Year after year, she scores extremely high on surveys and other professional assessments. She's not just a model for her profession. She's a model for the rest of us. She gives a damn.

The story brings to mind a common theme in many of my speaking engagements. It's also advice I offer to my employees and to other companies as a business coach and consultant. It's this: I don't care about revenue.

"What? Are you crazy?" That's what you're thinking, right?

You see, instead of focusing on revenue, I believe companies should focus on recruiting, rewarding, and empowering employees like Suitter. Businesses should care most about providing the best customer service possible. Shifting your focus in this way costs nothing and can improve the organization and everything around you. Some CEOs would probably disagree with my motto of, "Customer service is what counts, not revenue." They would probably insist that revenue is the most important component of any business. After all, without revenue you have nothing.

They have it backwards. It is excellence in customer service and product quality that drives revenue, not vice versa. If you provide the absolute best quality of product and customer service, the revenue will follow. And more than you might think. Remember the JavaPresse Coffee Company example in the last chapter, when they made just one simple change that did not cost a penny, but their revenue grew 800 percent?

That is one of the success factors of Give a Damn. If you give more to someone than they expect, they will want to do business with you over and over again. Although having a good product to begin with is important, this doesn't mean you have to provide more products. It means providing more attention, more service, more appreciation, and more follow-up for customers. In business, it's often the little touches that count the most.

It is not about revenue, it's about how to give a damn. If you give a damn, the revenue will come. Too many people think about the end result, rather than the actions that get you there: the added personal touches, the extra service and support, and the value-add that really drives revenue.

Service Professionals as Role Models

To give a damn means you value and respect others in every way. You value their time, feelings, background, perspective, and preferences—the entire package—even though you might disagree with them on certain issues or disapprove of their behavior.

Disagreement isn't a bad thing, but a closed mind is. You want to support and help customers in any way that you can. Isn't that what excellent customer service is all about in the business world? Too bad we don't experience more of this in our everyday lives and interactions with other people. High-performing customer service professionals like Suitter are not only models for their fellow customer service colleagues, they're also models for the rest of us.

As I stated in Chapter 2, technology has a dark side. Mobile devices, social media, and the internet are partly to blame for declining social-emotional skills like empathy, and studies support this. Today's technology and media drive an increased need for greater and more instant gratification, which leads to a decreased quality of interpersonal interactions. But people who provide high-quality customer service in their profession know how to overcome this.

Suitter's employer, Delta Air Lines, says it's just as important to recruit people who can overcome these toxic reinforcements as it is to give their people the tools to provide great customer service. Charisse Evans, Delta's Vice President for Customer Experience Integration, said it's critical for companies to be strategic about this.

"Delta recognizes the importance of investing in our people—from onboarding to future development," Evans told me in an email. "We also recognize that our people are the differentiator that can make an experience exceptional. That's why we are investing in programs that will continue to focus on the importance of creating memorable moments that can make a direct impact on customer experience."

People like Evans and Suitter have insights that we should all tap into. They show us what's possible. And they show us our responsibility. There are all kinds of tools and resources that can be used effectively to help develop a person's interpersonal skills. And change isn't just possible—it's necessary.

Let me once again discuss the principle-driven business approach of Ruark Chick, an executive at a major organization with hundreds of employees. Chick has some insights about this issue. He believes that accountability is a central tenet of high-quality service. Assessments of your effectiveness provide a foundation for your commitment to your work, which translates into happy clients.

"I'm not big on saying the word 'mistake.' I like looking back on a project and asking honestly whether it worked," Chick told me. "And accountability is about admitting what didn't work, asking what you're going to change moving forward, and then declaring that change to other folks so they're aware that change will occur."

He said that it starts with establishing a culture that drives people to being committed to clients and employees—to punch beyond the board, as they say in martial arts. A good team hits their target, but always aims for more.

Chick told me a story of a team member who not only fixed a client's IT problem per the support ticket, but also cleaned her keyboard and mouse. This is what Ruark refers to as "punching beyond the board." It makes a big difference in people's lives, even when the actions may seem small, because they are unforgettable. It's all about putting your "invisible signature" on your work. It's about taking pride in your commitment to client service.

"Why is it important that we provide an extra level of service for a service desk call? Why is it that we stay late to work with the accounting department on specialized coding to address a customer's request?" he said. "It's because we give a damn. We give a damn about our employees. We give a damn about our customers."

Chick sees the evidence of this success in surveys and direct feedback from clients.

People that give a damn take responsibility for their actions. This is especially important in customer service. If you make a mistake, own it and don't blame any circumstance that might have caused it; make it right and move on. Once, I had a client communicate to me about a specific product design. However, I interpreted her wishes incorrectly. I thought I'd done exactly as she asked, but I did not blame her for the mix-up. Instead, I took responsibility and made it right, even though our company lost money on the transaction.

Earlier in my career, I accepted blame as a representative of a company, and it incurred a personal financial cost for me. About four years into my career in IBM office equipment sales, I accepted the opportunity to move into selling computer systems as a new account sales rep.

I had gone through some additional training and I was about a year into selling systems when IBM came out with a new product called the AS/400. It was deemed an excellent product, and it was selling well. But there was one problem of which the marketplace was not yet aware: the internal processing power, or memory, was not adequate to handle specific functions, so it operated very slowly.

I had a customer, Mike, who managed multiple small hotels, and he was highly interested in purchasing the AS/400. I had a quota, and the sale would have gone a long way toward meeting it. However, at the end of the day, I told Mike not to order the AS/400 until IBM was able to fix the memory problem. He was a bit shocked and thanked me for being so honest with him. The commission I missed out on would have been substantial, but at the end of the day I did the right thing.

I became good friends with Mike, who turned out to be a neighbor of mine. Eventually he purchased IBM equipment for his business, and to this day he is still a loyal IBM customer. In the long term, both IBM and I benefited from the relationship that this short-term loss helped to build.

Finally, people that give a damn value other people's time and feelings. They have a sense of urgency toward others' needs. Give a Damn people are attuned to helping people and doing it quickly. They don't procrastinate. They get things done. This is a key difference between good and bad customer service. A sense of urgency means you want to get something done without delay. Those who act quickly, efficiently, and effectively are as successful in business as they are in their personal lives.

A priest and good friend of mine sent me an email that said, "Never underestimate the power of being nice to someone." It means you give a damn. The danger is in believing that being nice to someone will get you something in return. Then it becomes a self-serving behavior, because you expect something in return for what you did. Rather, we should do kind (altruistic) things for others just because we can.

How might you react to someone in a positive way? Periodically, I'll call a client just to say thanks. People tend to respond to my small outreach in a very positive way, especially since this is no longer commonplace. People who give a damn react in a positive but also giving way. My wife has a favorite quote that reads, "Do all the good you can, by all the means you can, in all the places you can, at all the times you can, to all the people you can, as long as you even can!"

Dealing with Negativity

After Hurricane Katrina, a few years into my tenure as president of the Louisiana Technology Council, we helped open a business recovery center. The center provided free phone and internet access, office furniture, and a computer to businesses who were affected by the storm. All these resources were available for a small fee of $150 per month.

There was one tenant, however, who didn't pay his fee for several months. All along he made promises, and we believed him, but he never came through. For months we tried to recover what he owed us without success, so we attempted to evict him. He then sued us because, according to the law, we could not evict anyone without going through a time-consuming and costly procedure. As we got closer to trial, he disappeared.

The LTC wound up losing six months of rent and paying thousands of dollars in legal fees. He took advantage of us. He didn't give a damn about what we did to help him through his loss. He only cared about taking advantage of the LTC, and he used the legal system to his benefit.

Some say that people who give a damn will usually be taken advantage of by those who don't. Unfortunately, these types of occurrences happen frequently. It's part of life. Yet, these situations should not deter anyone from maintaining a Give a Damn attitude. After all, even if you don't benefit from one instance, you will from countless others.

I have already mentioned that you should never expect anything in return when you give a damn, but I don't advocate that anyone be selfless to the point of being taken advantage of, either.

If another person repeatedly acts in a self-centered, flaky, lazy, disrespectful, entitled, or generally negative manner, the best remedy is to avoid them. Sometimes we know who these people are and it is not hard to single them out. By identifying and avoiding these people, we can concentrate our own Give a Damn attitudes on those who give a damn about us as well.

By the time children reach their teen years, they have probably already formed their Give a Damn mentality if they're going to have one. I believe that we were born to give a damn about each other. We all have an inner voice guiding us toward these principles; there's just a tremendous amount of noise that we must filter out to hear it. Filtering out all that noise, all that selfishness, and those toxic reinforcements, is a learned behavior. We must learn to listen in order to overcome.

Customer service professionals are in a unique position to show the world a better way. After all, they're the experts! I'm sure there are times when it doesn't feel to them like they're making a difference, especially on days when customer after customer is rude and disrespectful, but they are.

No one knows more about what it means to deal with negativity than Evans, who oversees customer service for an airline. "A lot of it is mindset and attitude," she told me. "If you make the personal choice to be all in and make it a great day, that can impact how you engage with customers and your colleagues."

Evans cited empathy as a major tool for dealing with the negativity inherent in airline customer service. "We also focus on putting ourselves on the other side of the counter and think about how we would want to be treated if we were the customer," she said. "There are small actions that can turn a negative to a positive, like simply listening or empathizing. A simple smile and gesture can also go a long way with a customer and show that we really care and want to make it a great experience."

I couldn't agree more.

If you're ever struggling in a customer service position, think back to when you were growing up. Remember the many people that helped you with schoolwork, your career, or other personal situations. In the vein of these people, great customer service doesn't have to be a dramatic gesture. It can be as simple as employing positivity in facial expressions, language, and tone, as well as valuing people's time. I believe this is called common courtesy, the sister of common sense. It is a caring and respectful attitude toward others.

Have you ever thought about offering a smile to everyone you meet, whether you know them or not? When someone does something nice for you, how do you feel? Not only does it make you feel good, but the person providing the act of kindness feels good, too. You both smile.

On the other hand, if someone is rude or mean to you, how do you feel? You might be surprised, bewildered, upset, or confused. But in all cases, it doesn't feel good. I can assure you the rude person isn't feeling too well, either.

When conflict is created, if it's not handled properly, it can result in something much worse. So, smile more often—like right now! Like the milk campaign, "It does a body good." Too often we underestimate the power of a touch, a smile, a kind word, a listening ear, an honest compliment, or the smallest act of caring, all of which have the potential to turn a life around.

Words are very powerful; they can either build others up or tear them down. Language choice not only makes a difference in how our listeners feel, but also in how we perceive a situation. For example, would you rather wear a jacket that is "old" or "vintage?" What about a neighbor who is "eccentric" versus one who is "crazy?" These words can be used to describe the exact same thing, but our outlook changes immensely based on which words we use.

The same is true with our actions when combined with words. For example, I can tell you that I love you in a soft and caring manner, or I can tell you that I love you in an aggressive tone of voice with my hands about to be clenched around your neck. Our tone of voice and gestures have a lot to do with how our words come across. In fact, they can sometimes be more important than the actual words spoken.

We need to watch what we say and be careful how we use our words and how we act when delivering them. We can always get our point across in a positive and caring way if we just put some thought into it *before speaking*.

When interacting with negative people, if you don't have the option to avoid them (which customer service professionals don't), try to keep in mind that they may have challenges in life that you aren't even aware of. Sometimes we need to give them the benefit of the doubt.

You don't know their full history or how it's affecting their behavior, but you can assume there's something in their experience worthy of empathy. You can't control their behavior, and their poor behavior isn't a reflection of you, so just accept the person and the interaction and try to stay above it.

When the interaction is over, whatever negative force is causing their bad behavior may continue to be a problem for them—but not for you.

Chapter 8 – Give a Damn in Your Community

There's a famous parable about an ancient king who, in the middle of the night, placed a boulder on a roadway near his palace. He then hid himself and watched to see if anyone would remove the huge rock. Some of the king's wealthiest merchants and courtiers came by and simply walked around it. Many loudly blamed the king for not keeping the roads clear, but none did anything to get the stone out of the way.

Toward evening, an exhausted peasant came along carrying a load of vegetables. Upon approaching the boulder, the peasant was struck with worry that someone might collide with the boulder during the night. He laid down his burden and tried to move the stone to the side of the road. After much pushing and straining, he finally succeeded.

After the peasant picked up his load of vegetables, he noticed a purse lying in the road where the boulder had been. The purse contained many gold coins and a note from the king indicating that the gold was for the person who removed the boulder from the roadway.

The peasant learned what many of us never understand: Obstacles in our path present Give a Damn opportunities to help others—and by taking them, we help ourselves.

Courtesy and Kindness

When working for the Louisiana Technology Council, I planned hundreds of events, including lunch-and-learn sessions on topics to help technology businesses grow. We brought in experts to give tips on different methods for raising capital, implementing new technology, or understanding the costs, benefits, and implementation of new business systems.

For these sessions, free food was provided for attendees. We asked people to register online so that we would know how many people were attending and therefore know how much food to order.

Invariably, many people registered and did not show up. They didn't even notify us that they weren't coming! We told the restaurant how many meals to prepare based on the number of registrations we received, so we still had to pay for each meal for no-shows. Wouldn't it have been common courtesy for them to tell us if they weren't coming, regardless of whether it was a free event? Was it just laziness, a lack of manners, or both? How would they feel if they were hosting the event, had 50 registrations, and no one showed up? That did not quite happen to us, but you get my point.

It is all driven by a self-centered attitude and not thinking about how their actions might affect others. I can understand such behavior in the case of an emergency, but these no-shows aren't a rarity. They happen all the time. It's just another example that demonstrates a don't Give a Damn attitude.

Part of the problem is that people are just oblivious to their surroundings. It's a condition of not thinking about the effect their actions might have on the people around them. Or, for that matter, the effect their actions might have on people that come after them. It's a classic case of out of sight, out of mind.

In the last chapter, I discussed the value of customer service. Serving others, being polite, taking responsibility, and showing respect costs nothing and can improve everything in an organization. Give a Damn people not only take a customer service approach in their workplace, they also apply it to their world at large.

There is a saying that we should give people more than what they expect, and I completely agree. But more importantly, we should give people more of what they *don't expect*. It is done indirectly, and people never will know it.

Let me explain. When you pick up a rusty nail in a parking lot, you are doing something that could affect someone in the future even though they will never be aware of it. If you decided not to pick up the rusty nail, it's likely someone would drive over it and get it lodged in their tire. They could eventually have a blow out, or, at the very least, have to get the tire repaired. And what if that someone was your mom?

The Give a Damn person would pick up the nail and throw it away so that no one will ever be harmed by it. It doesn't bother a Give a Damn person that no one will admire or reward his deed. He knows that anonymous good deeds are the best kind. There is no ego involved. I am confident that a Give a Damn person, one you have never met or known, has probably done something that impacted your life in a positive way, but there is no way of you ever knowing about it.

When a situation directly relates to us or to someone we care about, we normally and want to do something about it. When we get outside our internal domain of self-interest, many times we don't give a damn, but we should. We should all think about the effect a situation might have on someone—anyone!—and take the same Give a Damn action. If it helps, relate your action to someone close to you, such as a family member or mentor. This may motivate you to change how you think and act.

Diana, Princess of Wales, famously sent thank you notes for even the most minor acts of generosity. She once said, "Carry out a random act of kindness, with no expectation of reward, safe in the knowledge that one day someone might do the same for you." It is such a great statement! It's amazing what the power of kindness can do. Kindness allows us to connect to hearts, touch souls, and transform lives.

Remember what the priest said in the last chapter? "Never underestimate the power of being nice to someone."

When there is a catastrophic event in nature, it is truly remarkable how people give a damn to help others. They come out in droves to help without expecting anything in return. It seems that the direr the situation, the more people give a damn. After Hurricane Katrina, volunteers and donations poured into the city. The LTC was the beneficiary of thousands of dollars from individuals and other tech councils throughout the country. People came from all over and spent their vacations stripping away moldy drywall and helping to build new homes. And they helped people they did not even know!

Why is it that when something major happens to people, we truly want to help those in need? Do we feel guilty? Do we feel an obligation? Do we feel sorry for them? There is this overwhelming feeling of wanting help others because of what happened. We become compassionate and understanding, and we reach out because we think about how we would feel if such a thing were to happen to us. We relate.

It's sad that it takes a major disaster to bring out this kind of altruism. And it's even sadder that, once the catastrophe disappears from the media, it often disappears from people's minds and thoughts as well.

How great would it be if we all behaved with this generosity and compassion every day, and it became a habit and not an exception? It would be terrific! So why can't people give a damn like that all the time? I don't have an answer, but the fact that they demonstrate empathy, hard work, and positivity during moments of tragedy gives me hope that most people truly do give a damn. They just don't know how to do it all the time because they have not learned it as part of their everyday habits.

Sometimes, people do surprise me, like when I got to observe strangers giving each other more of what they *didn't* expect.

During a business trip, I found myself on a flight that had been completely booked, with only three single seats available that were scattered throughout the plane. A mother and her two small children were the last ones to board. As a result, all three had to sit in separate seats.

The attendant asked if there were three people in a row who would be willing to move so the family could sit together. One row agreed. They got up and went to separate seats. These three strangers clearly felt compassionate toward the kids being split up and how traumatic that might have been for them. The row of passengers understood the situation and demonstrated, with their collective action, how to give a damn. In so doing, they made one mother's life a whole lot better for that plane ride.

And guess what? Remember in Chapter 2, people who are religious live almost four years longer? Such altruistic acts can also help us live longer! In addition to the effect that our kindness has on others, kindness is great for our own health. There have been multiple scientific studies that emphasize this fact.

Stephen G. Post, the Founding Director of Stony Brook University's Center for Medical Humanities, Compassionate Care, and Bioethics, uncovered this trend years ago—and his research continues to drive it home. Based on his review and interpretation of evidence on the benefits of volunteering, he asserted that no other behavioral intervention is as beneficial for promoting health.

His 2017 review looked at research on people of all ages, as well as special populations, including those suffering from chronic pain and heart disease. He found reduced mortality and other benefits to be so universal that he recommended physicians prescribe volunteering to their patients. The sweet spot, his examination showed, is volunteering for 100 hours a year (roughly two hours a week).

"Prescribing or recommending helping attitudes and actions in patients or communities is a universally valid contribution to preventive medicine and to the treatment of a wide variety of illness conditions," Post wrote in his commentary. "As a professor in a department of family, population, and preventive medicine, I can think of no other behavioral interventions that are as beneficial."

We often focus on the benefits of eating healthy and exercising, but clearly the health benefits of simple kindness and helping others are just as significant. Give a Damn people who act with kindness and bring goodness into the lives of others live longer. Don't we all want that?

In these wonderful moments when another person bestows a kindness upon you that you didn't expect, don't let it pass by without creating a Give a Damn moment in return. When someone does something nice for you or gives you a gift or compliment, you should thank him and do it in a special way. This attitude of gratitude will help grow the Give a Damn herd.

Be thankful! The size of the nice thing that was done for you does not matter. Our society underestimates the power of the simple words "please," "thank you," and even "excuse me." These words still go a long way in any endeavor. It is amazing to me how many people never say these words anymore.

Personal handwritten thank you letters and notes are becoming a lost art because of the internet. Most of us probably now communicate our appreciation—if we do it at all—through email or text messages because it is easy and fast. This is better than nothing, but not as meaningful as a handwritten note. In the future, technology may make handwritten notes obsolete, but kids still need to be taught an attitude of gratitude at an early age. It shows you care and that you give a damn by thanking others for their kindness.

People should go the extra mile to thank their friends, associates, first responders, the military, and anyone else for that matter, because everyone wants to be appreciated.

Crime and Violence

I've talked a lot in this book about my personal brush with white-collar corruption during the Nagin administration. But crime has many other insidious forms.

As I was traveling to work one day, I heard news on the radio about a person who was crossing a long bridge over a body of water and threw two kittens out of a car window. One of the kittens managed to survive as it was found in a drain. The other did not.

The story was all over the news. How could anyone commit such a heinous act? Were the kittens too expensive to care for? Maybe the kitten thrower justified his actions based on not being able to take care of the kittens, but throwing them out of a car window is not the solution. Is this not common sense? You cannot convince me of any justification of this incident.

114

Would anyone think about throwing his own loving pet out of a car? I hope not! Once we love something, it is our natural instinct to protect it and fight for it—to give a damn. There was no consideration for the well-being of those kittens. This type of self-centeredness is ruining our society, and it's becoming more rampant every day.

The day after the kitten was found in a drain, a radio talk show host brought the subject up for people to call in and discuss. The question was, "How can anyone even *think* about doing something so barbaric?" The talk show host commented that, once the person was found, he should go straight to jail for a long time.

One caller said that, as a youngster, he did similar things, but had since reformed his ways because he found God. The caller said that he thought people were just inherently evil and that these kinds of things were ingrained into our psyche. It was human nature.

Apparently, some people believe that human beings are naturally violent, and that we have simply curbed our natural inclinations of violence in order to create a functional society. Are newborns already predisposed to violence in their DNA? Are we little more than animals living within a civilization?

I don't believe that humans are born with an instinct to hurt or kill others. How in the world could our species have lasted over the past 200,000 years without the instinct to care for others? I think it's more likely that people learn how to act from their environment. If caring for others is valued and modeled, then, in most cases, that will be the learned behavior.

There have been many instances in the past when some twisted leader or faction has tried to take over the world and failed. None of these so-called leaders or groups had a Give a Damn attitude. And guess what? They all eventually failed! Bloodthirsty or power-hungry ambitions have certainly been contributing causes to many revolutions throughout history, but people eventually saw through them and rejected these ideals.

Furthermore, what role does the environment play in how a newborn learns behavior? A ton! As I mentioned in Chapter 2, the three primary reasons for a rise in self-centered behavior are: a lack of a values-driven education in school and at home; toxic reinforcements caused by technology, the media, and pop culture; and a government driven by special interests.

I believe that learned selfishness, not human nature, is the primary cause of violence. Over time, this self-centeredness and ignoring of other people causes tension, and it grows like a cancer. And this selfishness, when triggered by petty arguments, erupts in unthinkable violent behavioral responses.

There is never a reason to physically fight someone. No one wins when a fight erupts. I am not talking about going to war or defending yourself in a dangerous situation, because that is a whole different ballgame. It's this competitive, must-win-at-all-costs attitude that creates a problem. And the stakes are higher than people think.

Although many of those involved with crimes have been affiliated with gangs or drugs, it is easy to see that the problem goes way beyond these factions. Often, the motives behind these crimes have been centered on trivial—and what I would call ego-driven—circumstances, such as maintaining one's status or saving face.

It's so sad to think that a commonly cited reason for violent behavior is trivial arguments. But a simple argument can indeed escalate to hatred and then murder. Too many murders in this country occur because two people get into an argument over something simple, such as money, status, a relationship, or even a parking spot.

Why is it that someone always has to win, and if they don't, they have to cause harm? Life is not a zero-sum game.

When you give a damn, you try to relate to what the other person is saying or feeling. Who wants to get hurt anyway? I have never been in a fight. I always try to look at the dynamics of what is going on and understand them before I react. And it's not easy. I attempt to relate to the other person by putting myself in their shoes and trying to understand why they are acting in such a way. Does that make me weak or wimpy? Nope. Mostly, I just know how to control my emotions and succeed in these types of challenging situations.

The best way to avoid a fight is to apologize and say something kind. It works every time. When you react with kindness in a highly charged situation, it diffuses the tension, even if it's just for a short moment. This does, however, take quick thinking and some practice.

In large part, technology is to blame for robbing us of skills like maintaining empathy in an emotionally charged situation. We need to spend more time interacting with people in all sorts of situations and less time watching screens.

As I noted in Chapter 2, the rapid growth of technology has played a huge and detrimental role in our behavior. I am not suggesting that technology is bad overall, but in this aspect, it is. There seems to be a growing cancer of apathy these days, which has led many people to forget about how to care for others. Many people have simply ceased or never learned to care about human life—sometimes not even their own.

Most people will admit that we have become desensitized by all the violence we see on TV, in video games, in movies, and in the world in general. Years ago, we would react in disbelief to violent actions or behaviors, such as shootings or bombings. Now it seems like we just acknowledge that it happened again, without much emotion.

Possible contributors to bad behavior that we have accepted as normal today— and which technology has made so readily available— include violent videogames that focus on killing and destruction, violent movies, pornography, and ultimate fighter sports programs.

Violence has been with our species throughout much of our evolution, and one only needs to visit the archaeological site of Pompeii to see that pornography also has ancient origins. But the availability of mobile devices and streaming technologies has made this graphic content so mainstream that it's affecting society in a new and terrible way.

Rowland Atkinson, Research Chair of Inclusive Societies at the University of Sheffield, and his colleague Thomas Rodgers refer to this content as "cultural zones of exception." In these zones, people can temporarily disregard the norms of civilized society to briefly live out their darkest fantasies. Their research considered some of the most extreme types of sexual and violent content available on mobile and screen media.

Their 2015 study argued that these zones legitimize the pursuit of any and all actions against anyone a player or viewer encounters. These media are coded and designed to permit any conduct desired (within the limits of computer programming, of course). Other people or characters in these zones become, by definition, subordinate to the whims and desires of the player or viewer.

Cultural zones of exception enable people to view or live out acts of violence without having to suffer the consequences of being witnesses or participants in real life. And these "moral holidays," as the authors describe the screen-based experiences in their study, are not supposed to affect us in any way? Does this pass the common-sense test? Absolutely not.

In time, people who frequently partake in this kind of violent entertainment become desensitized to it, requiring more and more extreme experiences to jump start that feeling. The more desensitized they become, the more normal it seems to them, and eventually this can become an obsession or addiction.

Those who market and promote simulated violence, such as in video games, are doing so because of financial gain, and they have no shame about glorifying the contents of their product. It's what the public wants, and that in of itself is a problem. And because they have high demand for their product, they do everything they can to amplify it to the world. They apply slick marketing, amazing design skills, and creativity to tap into people's darkest urges. They never decry the violence they depict except when they label it as for mature audiences only. Does anyone even know what a mature audience is? I don't. Is it based on how old you are? Maybe so, but the "mature audience" is encouraged to take delight and thrill in simulated brutality. Is this what mature people do?

Perhaps these "moral holidays" and "zones of suspension," seem harmless—or just a game. But they don't just lead young people to waste their time on video games rather than engaging in enriching activities. They can also become deadly, leading people to think that their worldview or frustration merits violent behavior. It may seem OK for them to take the life of another. I believe this is one of the contributing factors to three of the most extreme manifestations of violence today: gang violence, mass shootings, and terrorism.

There has to be a way to rein in this culture of violence. It is not an easy fix because changing a mindset is a monumental task. My hope is that this book can offer some solutions, or at least be a starting point for a solution. Am I a dreamer? Sure, but we have to start somewhere. And why not now? As the saying goes, the only people who change the world are the ones that are crazy enough to do so.

So, if we can change people's thinking, can we help change their behavior? I sure hope so.

There needs to be a broader understanding of what it means to give a damn and that success in life, in a school or work environment, or in a moment's argument should not come at the expense of others. Our youth need to understand the process and demands involved in working hard and obtaining wealth, and that it just doesn't happen overnight. They must understand that hard work, no matter how tedious it may seem at first, is a much better—and, ultimately, more profitable—choice than taking the quick, dirty, and life-threatening route. They need to understand that trivial grievances can be addressed in civil ways that benefit both parties, and they need to be given the social-emotional skills to de-escalate a conflict.

In late 2014, the FBI reported that mass shootings had been on the rise over the past 14 years. And they certainly continue. The mass shootings that occur all too often in the United States are often motivated by personal grievances related to the workplace, household, school, or other environment. Although we often dismiss the perpetrators as merely mentally ill or having suffered some type of traumatic experience in their life, this phenomenon is becoming all too common—almost like an epidemic. There has to be something more to it.

I am not discounting the fact that active shooters could have mental health issues that drive them to murder people for no apparent reason. What I am saying is that there has to be something else going on that turns these mental health issues deadly.

There is a point that I want to stop to emphasize here: the Give a Damn philosophy is not a substitute for psychological or medical treatment. Medication does a lot to help with mental health conditions. I sure wish society would treat mental health issues the same way that we treat physical health issues like high cholesterol or high blood pressure. When the physical body has a condition that medication treats, we are OK with that, yet we see things much differently when it comes to mental health. Mental health support is an integral and vastly important part of crime prevention.

But therapy, medication, and other evidence-based solutions are not a cure-all for violence in our society. I believe there must be a complementary intervention of principles as well.

So, here is my theory on most mass murders: They are based on the desire of perpetrators to seek fame or retribution and their willingness to go to any length to get it. These perpetrators feel that they have been in the shadows all their lives and no one cares about them. Often, the only attention they ever receive is negative: "You're not good enough," "You're stupid," "You're lazy," and so on.

They begin to believe that negative attention is the only way for them to get noticed. And what's a great way to gain the ultimate form of negative attention? In extreme cases, it's having one's face plastered across TV or the front pages of newspapers after committing a horrific crime like murdering people.

These people do not consider or care about the consequences of their actions when it comes to other human beings. They don't give a damn as to who gets hurt or dies as long as they receive the ultimate coverage. And once they finish their act, they often commit suicide, likely seeing themselves as going out in a final blaze of glory.

So, how does the media play a role in all of this? By exploiting and sensationalizing spree killings. Sure, they have to cover it. But frankly, they don't give a damn about the excessive coverage provided for this kind of violence. Why? Because it attracts viewers and ratings, and the better the ratings, the more money it will generate. Does such sensationalized coverage attract copycat acts? Common sense says yes, positively! But there's also data to back it up.

A group of social scientists from Arizona State University and Northeastern Illinois University found significant evidence for this phenomenon by applying a contagion model, in which "recent prior events increase the probability of another event happening in the future," to mass shootings. A similar contagion model has been applied to financial markets, social media, and other phenomena, but this study marked the first time it was applied to mass killings and school shootings.

In their 2014 study, the researchers found that mass shootings have a contagious effect for 13 days—when coverage, it seems to me, generally begins to die down—leading to more potential shootings within that timeframe. Although the authors noted that the study tested "contagion by whatever means," it seems to me that continued media coverage of violent acts has served as a model upon which others with the same sick mindset can shape their own behavior.

Both Seung-Hui Cho, the Virginia Tech shooter, and Adam Lanza, the perpetrator of the Sandy Hook massacre, were fascinated by the Columbine shootings, with Cho even going so far as to praise the shooters as "martyrs" in his final manifesto.

James Holmes, the Colorado movie theater shooter, was quoted during his trial as saying, "At least I'm remembered for doing something." There is something going on in a person's psyche other than mental illness for them to say something like this. That something is a thirst for attention regardless of the cost to others.

We must address our society's decline into this self-centered behavior if we ever hope to stop these terrible acts.

In addition to a search for fame or vengeance, mass violence is also used to coerce people and spread poisonous ideologies (i.e., terror). It seems to me that more and more individuals are placing less value on human life, whether it's their own or that of others. And it's not just a problem in the United States—it's global. This seeming disregard for life takes many forms, but terrorism is one of the most notable examples.

This is not to say that there has never been violence in the past—a quick glance at a history book easily disproves that—but it seems to be entering a new territory. New forms of violence, especially terror, are escalating and spiraling out of control.

It is certainly a topic that has become a fixture of our collective consciousness. The Islamic State group, al-Qaida, al-Shabab, and other groups have turned into household names, and for the wrong reasons. How to fight the spread of these groups seems to be a huge topic for every newspaper, talk show panel, and political debate in the country. No one has a good answer. My feeling is that one of the possible root causes of terrorism is the lack of a Give a Damn mentality in today's global society.

Although the proclaimed goals of terrorist groups are too numerous to list here, a common characteristic is that they use violence and fear to coerce a population into believing in a cause and doing what they want. They have ceased to give a damn about the wishes or the well-being of a population—although they will tell you otherwise—and focus only on achieving their self-serving goals through the most ruthless means possible.

It's all about them. They become so focused on their ideology that they forget what's really important: the people. All the people, not just those who they might call their own.

Are terrorists born this way? Absolutely not. Everyone in the world is born free from hate or malice. Despite the terrible twos, no one ever sees a 2-year-old and says, "He is violent." They are not terrible because they are violent; 2-year-olds are just difficult to live with because they are exploring, learning, and pushing boundaries.

And they continue to learn. What they learn today—and from so many different factions than ever before—will set the stage for who they will become tomorrow. They learn from parents, society, friends, mentors, schools—everything. As they grow older, their innocence is transformed and their adult behavior is based on most of their childhood experiences.

Throughout this book I underline the importance of education. Education from all sources is what shapes young learners into the type of adults they become. Those who receive moral, scholastic, and character-based education usually become quality people. They understand right from wrong. They develop traits critical for understanding good behavior and values, including why coercion and violence are wrong. They understand that the mission of a terrorist is to advance an extremist ideology at the expense of others, and they learn that it's wrong.

Unfortunately, in many parts of the world, children grow up in poverty with no real hope of an education in any sense of the word. They lack both the formal education needed to lift themselves out of poverty and, more importantly, the moral teaching to appreciate the value of human life. As a result, they become easy targets for those who wish to exploit their lack of education and turn them into fighters for a cause they barely understand.

They are offered a way out—a way to support something that they believe significantly raises their worth. You can see how easy it is to take a down-and-out young person with a limited understanding of morals, values, religion, or politics and influence them to fight for a cause. My guess is that the terrorist doesn't really call it terrorism. Rather, they see it as a fight for a just cause that, in reality, is a misguided one.

One example of this is how the Taliban gained influence in Afghanistan and Pakistan. Using both traditional and modern media channels, the Taliban used propaganda tactics to exploit incidents or issues, connecting them with seemingly related historical information, to provoke the local people to stand up for violence. In 2010, Osama bin Laden hadn't yet been found, coalition and Afghan government forces were increasing offensive operations against the Taliban, and casualties of innocent Afghan civilians were regularly reported.

At the time, Danish Karokhel, Director of the first internationally recognized independent news agency of Afghanistan, Pajhwok Afghan News, explained that the Taliban used misinformation for coercion. "Ninety percent of the information that the Taliban provide to the media is false: when only one Afghan soldier gets killed in an attack, the insurgents call the media and claim that 10 foreign soldiers are killed," he told the Huffington Post. The Taliban frequently provided their own interpretations of events, which people could not verify but were still believed. They positioned themselves as experts in religion to gain more power over the population.

Terrorism is a selfish act. So is every crime. Violent behavior in individuals stems from feeling a lack of control, self-esteem, and appreciation—and above all, a lack of hope. Egocentricity can and will destroy you, if not kill you.

So, how do we stop all this violence? It's going to be very difficult because everyone needs to give a damn, whether they are consumers, the media, politicians, neighbors, teachers, or peers. We all have to be on the same page because our success will depend upon the weakest link.

Having a Give a Damn attitude can help stop violence before it starts. Why? Because many perpetrators of violence feel that no one cares about them. If a person was surrounded by Give a

Damn people, don't you think they would acquire a Give a Damn mentality themselves? Don't you think they would feel appreciated? Don't you think society would be a lot better off?

A nurturing Give a Damn society can definitely influence people to make positive and correct choices. People will feel better about themselves and others. Give a Damn people think about the value of human life above all other things. They also take into consideration the long-term consequences of their actions. If we build a society of people who have internalized these values, we can certainly help reduce or stop violence before it starts.

Consumers need to give a damn about the kind of entertainment we choose to watch and participate in for ourselves and our children. We need to make a conscious decision to stop watching excessively violent movies and to not buy our children video games with a primary purpose of killing as many people as possible.

Parents need to limit screen time, internet, and phone usage, and instead send their kids out to play. Taking hikes, playing pickup sports, having a picnic ... remember that?

Media outlets need to stop sensationalizing active shooter incidents, and we need to stop tuning in to this excessive coverage. Networks are aware of their viewership and if enough of us tune them out, they will hopefully start covering other things.

If we start to give a damn and become selective with our media choices, we can change the current landscape of news and entertainment. And if we start leading our lives with principles, we will have a long-term and global impact on the safety of our communities. Everyone needs to give a damn!

We need all the solutions available to us—from access to mental health services to smart and effective policies limiting access to weapons of mass murder—but we also just need a less self-centered society. Too many people, especially those who would throw kittens out of a speeding car or commit brutal acts of terrorism, just don't give a damn about anyone but themselves.

I don't see the kitten-throwing or the frequency of heinous acts of mass killing as proof of evil. I see them as evidence that society is going down the wrong path. Crimes like animal cruelty, theft, and even murder are rooted in attitudes and behaviors that can be changed.

I know it's true because each day you can find countless instances of humans showing great displays of kindness, altruism, and elevation of spirit—all Give a Damn characteristics.

I firmly believe that Give a Damn is already built into everyone's psyche. It just needs to be brought out.

Chapter 9 – Give a Damn in Government

In 1918, a baby boy was born into the Madiba clan in a village in what would become South Africa. The boy grew up hearing elders tell stories of their ancestors' brave resistance. And these stories instilled in him a sense of his own obligation to serve his people. That little boy was Nelson Mandela.

Many years later, Mandela founded the African National Congress to resist apartheid, and he would toil for many years as a political prisoner. But eventually this astounding commitment to freedom would earn him a Nobel Peace Prize and a firm legacy as a hero of government reform. He sure paid the price, though. Mandela transformed South Africa from a country controlled by the white minority to a democratic and free society. In the process, he became a model for servant leadership throughout the world. He is recognized as a tremendously influential and life-long advocate for human rights.

Although he worked tirelessly for the causes of freedom and empowerment, Mandela was a servant. And he was proud to be a servant, despite suffering greatly in the process. He served others like few people in this world find the strength, stamina, and passion to do. And in 1994, in a moment of triumph for all who care about the public interest, Mandela became president in the country's first general election open to all races.

We all can't be Mandela. However, we can certainly try our best to imitate him to some degree. We should all make it our mission in life to find a purpose and to find a means of serving others in big or even small ways. We have a responsibility as citizens to work to improve the country we love. This is what it means to really give a damn.

I believe that changes are vastly needed in America's governing institutions. This chapter will outline the two domains in which change is needed the most: special interest groups' influence on our government and the legal system. I believe these are key reasons behind why we fail to prioritize education, our country's most valuable public investment in the future.

Public Interest Over Special Interests

Our founding fathers worked together for the betterment of society. They envisioned a society comprised of individuals and groups who would be free to act and worship as they pleased and speak their minds. But today, our society is transitioning into people speaking and working solely towards their own interests. This causes them to judge or even condemn anyone who dares to think differently, because they view any difference in viewpoint as a threat to their own interests.

Special interest groups play a big role in both politics and business. Some are member-based (representing the interests of a group of people with something in common), like the AARP or the National Rifle Association. Business interest groups, on the other hand, include the U.S. Chamber of Commerce, the American Marketing Association, and many others. There are probably hundreds, if not thousands, of groups in each category. Yet, do we truly understand the extent to which these groups shape our public or business policies, let alone our individual lives? Probably not.

I am not saying that all special interest groups are bad. They are not. The problem is that the good ones give a damn, while many others do not.

Politicians often try to cater to the needs of special interest groups, and it's not hard to understand why they do this. It is for votes and money. If one of these groups were to really give a damn, then in most cases their advocacy would consider the well-being of all citizens rather than just what is most beneficial for their members.

There have been many studies on the power that special interest groups have over public policy. One well-known study is that of political scientists Martin Gilens of Princeton University and Benjamin Page of Northwestern University.

Although many studies had previously tested whether America's policymaking process is truly democratic, Gilens and Page were the first to use a single statistical model to calculate the amount of influence held by various stakeholder or special interest groups. Their 2014 study demonstrated that economic elites and special interest groups have a much greater sway over public policy than the average citizen.

This certainly makes sense. As an individual you can make a difference, but collectively—and with lots of money—we have a huge influence. Gilens and Page noted that the preferences of economic elites are sometimes aligned with those of average citizens like you and me. It leads to what is termed coincidental representation: The wishes of the average citizen are fulfilled without them having had any kind of meaningful or direct influence on the process.

But here's where it goes wrong. Gilens and Page's study showed that the preferences of member-based special interest groups are rarely aligned with those of the larger public. For example, membership groups representing gun owners tend to take stands that run counter to the desires of the average American. The study further showed that the preferences of business-oriented groups have a negative correlation with the preferences of both median-income and affluent citizens. The influence of both kinds of groups is pretty substantial.

"When the preferences of economic elites and the stands of organized interest groups are controlled for, the preferences of the average American appear to have only a minuscule, near-zero, statistically non-significant impact upon public policy," they wrote.

Gilens and Page found that—to no surprise—any policy change is hard to make. Even when interests are aligned, there's a strong bias toward the status quo. Change is simply hard to come by.

But strong support among both interest groups and affluent Americans increases the likelihood of making a change. In the data set the researchers used, examples of policies that had strong support and still failed included increased educational spending for K–12 and college support.

You can guess from my previous discussion of Louisiana's Stelly Plan that I consider this to be a tragedy. I believe that much of the money we spend on welfare programs and corporate subsidies should be funneled into education instead.

The interest group debacle is even more disturbing after the 2010 Supreme Court decision in the case of *Citizens United v. the Federal Election Commission.* The case stemmed from a 2008 film critical of Democratic presidential candidate Hillary Clinton that the conservative non-profit Citizens United wanted to air and promote during an election advertising blackout period.

The court found that, since political spending falls under constitutionally protected free speech, the government can't keep corporations, non-profits, or unions from spending their own money on election-related communication.

The Citizens United ruling further amplified our country's special interest group problem to unprecedented levels because it legalized unlimited independent expenditures by unions, corporations, and non-profits in favor of a candidate or party. The court decided that defining corruption as anything other than giving money to an office or politician in return for a favor was a violation of the First Amendment.

The court found that, as long as these entities were only contributing money to support or oppose a political campaign and were not directly involved with the office holder, campaign finance restrictions did not apply. Seriously? As a result, the Supreme Court opened the door for a massive injection of money into subsequent political campaigns without almost no restrictions.

This gave anyone with enough money and inclination the ability to form a super political action committee. Super PACs may accept unlimited amounts of money from individuals, groups, or businesses as long as they refrain from being directly involved with a candidate.

Direct individual contributions to a candidate are still limited (based on the Bipartisan Campaign Reform Act of 2002), so no one can write a million dollar check and mail it to their candidate of choice. But the Supreme Court gave corporations, non-profits, unions, and interest groups the ability to collect and spend as much money as they see fit to independently advocate for a candidate. How does this pass the common-sense test? It's just not right.

At the time that I wrote the first edition of *Give a Damn*, I was alarmed by this decision. Citizens United seemed to open a big can of worms because it set the precedent for rulings that have further undermined campaign finance law. For several years now, there has been vigorous debate about how much of an impact this ruling has had on elections, but the principle of my objection still rings true.

Those in favor of Citizens United and other similar decisions argue that money does not necessarily guarantee a win for a certain candidate, which is probably true. They also argue that spending in favor of a campaign does not influence a candidate's behavior once elected, which is probably not true.

If a group finds a candidate that already supports their interests, why wouldn't they pour massive amounts of money into getting them elected? That is certainly not a bad thing if, and only if, it supports the well-being of the country and its citizens.

But let's use some common sense here. For instance, if I had no money and wanted to run for office, would I have a snowball's chance of winning? No way.

Now let's say my campaign had been bolstered by a billion dollars in donations, would I have a better chance of winning? Of course I would. Would I be indebted to those who provided me with a billion dollars to win my campaign? Of course I would. The problem is that the return of favors may be (and sometimes are) done for the wrong reasons.

If I were running for office and someone (or the masses) donated zillions of dollars to my campaign, I would make it very clear that any decision I made would be based on what is right for the country. My decisions would not be driven by an obligation to give political favors to whoever gave me the most money or to secure my re-election for another term. I know it's not that simple, but its common sense and the right thing to do. It's probably why I would never get elected anyway. Besides, my wife tells me that I would never get elected because I am too nice—and that is why she loves me!

Now here is the next interesting question: If a special interest group knew that a Give a Damn politician would always make the right decision but he might go against them, would they still pour money into getting him elected? Who would want to support my campaign (unless they were a true Give a Damn person or organization) if I did not support what they wanted when I knew it was wrong? What do you think?

I think that most would agree that many politicians make decisions for two reasons: to get votes that will enable them to stay in office and to secure future funding. They are not as concerned about what is in the best interest of the people, although they will tell you differently. Rather, they are most concerned about what is in the best interest of those with money and influence and how it might directly affect them. It would take a unique politician to give a damn for the whole rather than a piece. Therefore, special interest groups win.

Most Americans share my concern. A 2018 poll by the Pew Research Center revealed that a large majority (77 percent) of Americans want to see limits on the money that both individuals (which is somewhat in place now) and organizations (special interest groups) can spend on political campaigns. And nearly two-thirds (65 percent) feel optimistic that new laws could help to reduce the role of money in politics. I agree, because money influences people to make the wrong decisions for the wrong reasons. Money is power, and most of the money that is raised for politicians comes from special interest groups. There is no argument in that.

In the Supreme Court decision regarding Citizens United, as well as other cases, the trend has gone toward allowing an unlimited amount of money into politics. Simple common sense says this is not a good thing because it opens the door for too many questionable decisions to be made.

Serving our country's citizens and doing right is what it should be all about. And using common sense would be quite helpful as well.

The Legal System

The legal system is also to blame for people who don't give a damn. We have become such a litigious society, which has caused us to become more focused on what we can gain at the cost of others as opposed to what is right or wrong.

Money influencing the decisions of politicians isn't the only area in which special interest groups hold power. They also use litigation when necessary. This is not always a bad thing, as it can sometimes be the only way for a disadvantaged group to gain their rights.

A prime example of this is when the NAACP used litigation to fight for the desegregation of schools in *Brown v. Board of Education of Topeka*. This landmark civil rights ruling overturned the Supreme Court's previous "separate but equal" precedent, which had forced black children to participate in an inferior education system for 60 years.

However, there seems to be an alarming trend of litigation being used by groups with significantly less lofty goals. These modern special interest groups not only argue their cause through a well-funded army of lawyers and experts, but also make massive donations toward electing judicial candidates that they deem favorable to their cause.

In the post Citizens United era, this has only gotten worse. According to the Brennan Center for Justice at New York University School of Law, special interest groups' domination of state supreme court elections had been increasing for past 15 years but more recently saw a dramatic spike. In the 2013 to 2014 election cycle for state supreme courts, contributions from interest groups increased to a record 29 percent of total spending! A whopping 21 out of the 23 contested seats were won by the candidate who received the most money.

"Spurred in part by the U.S. Supreme Court's 2010 ruling in *Citizens United v. FEC*, special interests are increasingly taking out their own ads and sponsoring other election materials in judicial races rather than contributing directly to candidates," according to a 2015 report published by the non-partisan center.

Is this how we want to decide our judiciary?

A Citizen's Responsibility

Earlier in this chapter I discussed the fact that the majority isn't always right, that special interests are rarely aligned with the interests of the public, and that many politicians are corrupted by money. But if everyone gave a damn, we could trust majorities with the vote, we could trust interest groups with political influence, and we could trust politicians to make the best decisions and laws.

So, where do we start? How do we return to a democracy in which laws are made for the people, instead of allowing politicians to succumb to the pressure of special interest groups?

It's so tempting to say, "Let the people decide, not the politicians." However, there is a catch. It's true that many special interest groups distort our political system in an unhealthy way, but the majority isn't always right either.

Sometimes people make decisions irrationally or based off of incorrect information. What comes to mind is Henrik Ibsen's famous play, *An Enemy of the People*. In this play, the majority of the townspeople override a doctor's report that a hot spring resort in their town was contaminated. They incorrectly and, for the wrong reason, decided to keep and promote a severe public health hazard. They never asked the question, "What's the right thing to do?"

The characters in Ibsen's play did not give a damn. They made a self-serving decision to the detriment of others. They did it for selfish reasons. The consequence of doing the right thing was going to be quite painful to their community, so they justified making the wrong decision because it was right for them.

The majority can become extremely destructive when it is driven by self-serving motives. This is why we need to shape our society into a Give a Damn society that is responsible enough to serve the greater good.

Just like in the play, in a lot of real-world cases you must deal with unreasonable and self-centered people. But the Give a Damn premise, not simply the opinion of the majority, should be the overriding factor in decision-making.

I am not professing this to be easy. It will require a major overhaul of our current political system and the whole method of how each of us thinks. Someone needs to step up and lead this charge for change because we just can't just sit around and wait for it to happen.

Sure, legislative change is needed for special interest groups to work differently and to help in this process. But the change won't last if only campaign finance laws are addressed. Everyone in America needs to do what we can to instill an attitude of doing right.

To quote astrophysicist Neil deGrasse Tyson, "I dream of a world where the truth is what shapes people's politics, rather than politics shaping what people think is true." It is a very profound aspiration, but all it would take is for everyone to give a damn.

The question is this: Can we fix these problems to create a more informed public and a more democratic society? Only if we all (or a clear majority of us) were to have a Give a Damn attitude and mindset.

Impossible? I don't think so. Impractical? Maybe. But we have to start somewhere!

My personal journey as a citizen taking a stand against government corruption in New Orleans was a transformational moment for me. It put my family and me through the ringer, but it also opened my eyes to the possibilities for change.

After the Louisiana Technology Council project team went public with our findings, the city demanded that we provide them with a full report, which we did a few days later in a face-to-face meeting. We provided a 15-page breakdown of the processes we used and the findings we uncovered.

Upon delivery of the report, the city wanted their data back within 24 hours. Prior to being fired, we had assembled about 500 of the approximately 18,000 items missing from Nagin's email store before we had to stop processing the data. When I got the city's demand for their data to be returned, I knew the risk of complying with the Nagin administration's demands. Who could I trust if I gave the data back to them and did not keep a copy? It would be gone forever, and all our work would have been for naught.

I immediately notified the FBI of the city's demands. I asked them to subpoena the data from the LTC as soon as possible so that we could relieve ourselves of any additional responsibility. My goal was to make sure that the data was in the hands of an entity that could ultimately determine if it demonstrated any wrongdoing. Meanwhile, a meeting was set up with the city the next day to provide them with the computer that had the recovered stored data, along with a back-up hard drive.

If we went into that meeting without a subpoena from the FBI, I would have had to keep a copy of the data, but who would I have given it to? Fortunately, I did not have to answer that question. The morning before our meeting with the city, the LTC received a subpoena and boy, was I relieved! The data was picked up by the FBI, who asked me not to tell the city that they had it. I did not ask why, but agreed.

Joining our project team for our meeting with the city was a lawyer that provided pro bono legal services to the LTC. We were a non-profit organization who could not hire a full-time lawyer for this case. When we arrived at city hall, the media was in full force, but we did not talk to them.

We walked into the conference room and there were no less than six people—mostly attorneys, some of whom came all the way from Washington, D.C., to participate—present on behalf of the city. I thought, "Really? A contingent of lawyers to fight a small non-profit tech group?"

We had some short discussion on various topics, and then they asked me this question: "Does anyone else have the data that you are returning to the city?" I told them that I could not answer the question, but they demanded a response. After they continued to press, I excused myself from the room, called my contact at the FBI, and got the green light to give a straightforward answer.

I went back in the room and said, "I have been told that I can tell you who else has a copy of the data. The only entity that has a copy of the data is the FBI."

Everyone in the room went silent. It seemed that way for an hour but was probably only five seconds. The "oh ****" expressions on their faces were priceless! After the discussion resumed, we provided them with the data. We agreed with their request to not talk to anyone else about the case, especially the media. Then, they escorted us out through a set of stairs at the rear of the building so we could avoid the press.

Shortly thereafter, the city released a statement that the LTC had admitted that our work was flawed and that the results of our recovery were wrong. The media told me about this statement, which I absolutely denied, stating that we stood behind our processes and results.

But Nagin just poured it on. He said we were only after our "15 minutes of fame" and speculated that we lacked the expertise for the job. He accused our project team of using "flawed" methods to reach "invalid" conclusions.

For the LTC's part, we considered the project—to the extent that we were allowed to proceed—a huge success. The target for recovery was calendar items and email from the primary server that was replaced in 2008. It's true that we were not able to assemble a substantial amount of email before we were fired by the city, but we were on the right track and we got all the data. Several years of calendar and email items were restored and delivered to the city and several irregularities were uncovered.

We reported to the city, the FBI, and the public the nature of the irregularities, and we made it crystal clear that we believed they warranted further investigation. We noted in our report that the mayor's sent emails are "the most relevant electronic record of his work in city hall including his contacts with constituents, contractors and other elected officials." And yet, every sent email was automatically deleted once it was delivered.

We also noted in our report that bit-level forensics could recover parts of the missing communications and emphasized our desire to perform that analysis. Unfortunately, we never got the chance.

We'd already had to watch our reform-minded mayor seemingly forget his own integrity. We had to resort to underbidding as a way to steer a municipal contract to a local firm. And after finally landing a contract with the city, which was skeptical of its own community's expertise, and working so hard to prove ourselves by finding a way to piece the trashed data back together, seeing him drag the quality of our work through this media firestorm just felt like we were being bullied. Of course, that wasn't the end of it.

Shortly thereafter, the city sued the LTC. They stated that we had violated our nondisclosure agreement. This was false. The LTC project team maintained strict confidentiality throughout the data recovery process. In accordance with our non-disclosure agreement, we never provided any restored email or calendar information to the media.

We only provided general information on our processes and results, including the deliberate deletion of public information in a manner that we were concerned might have violated the law. It seemed like a matter of our team's integrity to share those general conclusions with the public.

At the end of the day, Nagin was convicted on 20 counts of bribery, wire fraud, tax evasion, and other corruption charges. He was sent to federal prison for 10 years—a light sentence in many people's view. The prosecutor said Nagin sold his office for personal gain, including lavish trips and other bribes from city contractors.

I had warned my project team from the very beginning that we might never get paid, and we never did. To this day, I am convinced that the only reason that the city hired the LTC was not because we were the low bidder, but because the city did not think we were capable of doing the work.

I may never know how much our work helped investigators and prosecutors do their job. But at least I know that we demonstrated that the New Orleans business community doesn't just have the expertise to solve complex technical problems. We also have the values and moral courage to stand up for the best interests of the city we love.

Chapter 10 – Changing from the Inside

Altruism is a behavior. It's your actions performed for the benefit of others. But it's also an inner directive and change. It should never be forced. You want it to be natural, because then it's easy. Therefore, you must reorient yourself to want to help others first for the behavior to follow.

Altruism is a delicate balance. Effective altruism isn't an extreme. You should never get lost in an obsession with your own identity as an altruistic person; in my mind, that would be unhealthy. And I would never tell someone to act with such selflessness that they would lose sight of their own self-worth or preservation. Again, it's about balance. To me, it's about being able to serve others in a way that also makes you happy. Selfless behavior leads to a happier and longer life.

Finding that balance for what altruism really means to you is critically important. Making this inner change moves the needle further away from a self-fulfilling prophecy of self-centered behavior. Mind you, it's not easy and it's not an overnight process.

Don't expect anything in return. You should never feel entitled to expect it back. Too many times people do something generous expecting something in return. However, that return might not come in a form you expect or feel entitled to. It might not even be tangible; however, trust and kindness will be repaid in one form or another.

From altruism flows the rest of the Give a Damn values:

Empathy: To fight narcissism within ourselves, so that we can value others and behave with regard for others—even those we don't know

Teamwork: To work hard within a group—whether in your business, for your country, or for the Give a Damn movement—putting the goals of your institution above your individual desires

Commitment: To honor your word, no matter the circumstance.

Hard work: To create your own good luck and find your own success

Integrity: To fight the temptation to compromise the values that Give a Damn encompasses, to adhere to the right conduct and right way, to maintain consistent moral principles, and to feel a sense of pride in your mom's (or God's) eyes and your own

Courage: To maintain a Give a Damn attitude even in tough circumstances and to follow your conscience instead of following the crowd; to never try to justify the wrong conduct because it might be convenient or easy

Respect: To treat others with dignity, compassion, and understanding no matter who they are or what they might believe in; to treat others the way you would want to be treated

Kindness: To behave with warmth toward people we meet and to seek good for others

Positivity: To see the best in humanity, expect the best out of each and every day, radiate energy that lifts people up, and smile as much as possible

Honesty: To tell the truth, regardless of its consequences

Accountability: To hold ourselves to high standards—and take responsibility when we fall short

Gratitude: To show appreciation for the people and circumstances that support us

These are words that we need to live by. Give a Damn encompasses all of these values and then some. But these are nothing more than words unless we actually act on them. Our greatest challenge is to behave according to our beliefs and one of these beliefs should be to give a damn.

We must practice it on a daily basis. We must make it our attitude and live by it totally. Internalizing these 12 values will turn you into a person of true quality.

Gaining Awareness

The author and evangelical pastor Charles R. Swindoll wrote this reflection on attitude:

> The longer I live, the more I realize the importance
> of choosing the right attitude in life.
> Attitude is more important than facts.
> It is more important than your past;
> More important than your education or your financial situation;
> More important than your circumstances, your successes, or your failures;
> More important than what other people think or say or do.
> It is more important than your appearance, your giftedness, or your skills.
> It will make or break a company.
> It will cause a church to soar or sink.
> It will make the difference between a happy home or a miserable home.
> You have a choice each day regarding the attitude you will embrace.

And so it should be with you. Are you positive or negative? We are in charge of our attitude. Awareness of both our own thoughts and our impact on others is the first step toward developing a Give a Damn mentality. No one else will do it for you, although your resulting actions can have a profound effect on someone else. You just need a certain mindset to make it happen.

Changing a mindset is a huge challenge. Our thoughts and feelings shape every aspect of our lives. These thoughts and feelings are shaped by everything that goes on around us and they also determine our response to any situation. The thoughts that currently or eventually lead us to selfish and irresponsible behaviors are poisonous. But they are also often so subtle that we are not even aware of them.

As we grow up, we develop ideas about ourselves and about others, and we also develop habits. These ideas and habits can vary greatly depending on our individual experiences. However, no matter how they are formed, once they are in place, they can be very difficult to change. Ask smokers who want to quit how tough it is. Yet, if you are determined and focused, you can change.

Perhaps there have been situations in your life where you have thought, "It is OK, because no one will notice what I am about to do." This mentality can range from things as minor as tossing a cigarette out of a car window to major wrongs, such as stealing. The overall thought process is that since no one will see you do it, you justify it as being OK. We have to stop thinking this way.

The first step is to become aware of these poisonous thoughts. Give a Damn boils down to how we think and how that thinking translates into our behavior.

As you become conscious of your poisonous thoughts, you will also become conscious of your conscience. We all have a little voice inside of us whispering to do the right thing. We tend not to hear it or to ignore it, when all we need to do is listen to it. Over many years, you may have been guided by negative influences. But don't let these influences stop you from thinking about how you can give a damn.

As hard as it may be to start, we just need to listen to that inner conscience voice and think about doing more of the right things. Once you are more aware of your thoughts and their influence on your actions, you can begin to have more control over both of them.

We have to maintain a positive attitude and not feel that others are out to get us. We cannot always win. We cannot become bitter when we can't control everything that happens around us. We cannot be jealous of people who seem to have more than us.

This process of becoming aware of your thought processes and paying more attention to your inner voice of integrity takes time and effort, but I promise you it is worth it. It is worth it for our country and for the world.

We should actively become more aware of the people around us. Observing others and how they behave is the best way to learn how to give a damn. Start making mental notes of those who do and do not give a damn. When you observe someone who gives a damn, you begin to internalize the actions that really count.

You don't have to write it down—although it would be even more effective if you did—but be aware of it. Do this for a whole week and see what you come up with.

When making your observations, ask yourself these questions: What is the ratio of people around you who do and do not give a damn? In which situations are Give a Damn attitudes common, and in which are they lacking? What can you do to improve this ratio?

I'm not encouraging you to judge others—quite the opposite! Try putting yourself in another person's shoes in tough situations. For instance, consider a pregnant woman who smokes. If the pregnant woman put herself in the other person's shoes, she would think about the unborn baby in her womb. Her smoking may lead to premature birth, low birth weight, or an increased likelihood for her baby to die from sudden infant death syndrome. I know she wouldn't want that.

At the same time, if we put ourselves in the mother's shoes, we might think about how challenging it is to quit smoking. We might consider how complicated, stressful, or even traumatic her life might be going through that. After all, we don't know her.

Even from the strongest women I've had the joy to know, I've heard that pregnancy is tough, and quitting smoking is one of the hardest things you can do as well. So you see, giving a damn doesn't mean judging people. It means to expect better from yourself and others, but also offer compassion and understanding.

This is really, really important to understand. Think about putting yourself in someone else's shoes when it comes to a situation and how you would want that person to act toward you. Think about how you would feel being that other person and you will have a much better understanding of how to proceed. You will find that your actions and understanding will be quite different when considering another's perspective.

As you gain more empathy for others and their perspectives, you will find that you will begin to make fewer excuses for yourself. When you give a damn, you do the right thing. Choosing to do the right thing is not always easy. But by doing it over and over again, it eventually becomes a part of you.

So, as you continue to consciously observe the world through the Give a Damn lens, note which people perform actions that show that they really give a damn. You will be wowed by it. They are not greedy or self-centered. They lead by example. They are humble and let their actions speak for themselves. They are servants. They work with people and for people, and they don't feel like anything is beneath them. They are team players. They do things that are right, even though it might be to their detriment. They listen to their conscience. These are the people you want to be around.

Give a Damn people are leaders who want to help others, even if it means putting in the extra work. It's just the right thing to do. If you know how to give a damn, leaders will come to you for help, which now makes you a leader as well!

As a result of observing others and their actions, you will become more aware of your own actions and words in certain circumstances. You will then start asking yourself, "Did I give a damn?"

I'll bet most of you can think of hundreds of ways you did not give a damn at certain points in your life, and it was probably because you were not aware of what you were doing or might have done. At the same time as we are observing others, we need to be aware of our own thinking process, biases, and the insecurities and fears that impede our progress.

Soon you will be able to analyze your actions before they occur and bring them up to a Give a Damn standard. So many of the selfish and destructive actions we take today are also impulsive. This world is so fast-paced. When faced with a choice, slow down and think and you will make a better decision.

For example, lying is often a gut-level and fast defensive reaction to a perceived danger. When you feel the desire to hide the truth, take the time to consider what you will get out of a trusting relationship versus the short-term gain you might get out of evading the truth. Generally, the short-term benefit of telling a lie is outweighed by much greater and more painful future consequences. Don't let it happen.

Think before you act! Review the ethics of planned decisions or activities before implementing them. Use the questions below (or similar ones) as your litmus test. Answering no to one or more of the following questions would suggest a need for you to change your thinking. If you cannot, maybe you might need to seek counsel or advice from appropriate sources.

- Is it legal?

- Does it comply with appropriate rules and guidelines?

- Is it in sync with my personal or organizational values that relate to others?

- Will I be truly comfortable and guilt-free if I do it?

- Does it match my stated commitment to do the right thing and make the right decisions?

- Would I do it to my family or friends?

- Would my mother approve?

- Would the most ethical person I know do it?

- And perhaps the best question of all is this: Would I be perfectly OK with someone doing it to me?

For most of us, taking these steps will mean making some conscious changes. Slowly but surely it will become a natural process. Be patient. Over time you will make progress. No one is perfect, but the more we give a damn, the better our world becomes.

Finding the Love Within

So now that you have become more aware, what do you do next?

You can reorder your long-held priorities and change your long-held habits by searching for a life purpose that trumps pure self-interest. I believe that each life is meant to serve a purpose. Again, I'll ask this question: Why did God put you on this earth? Most people cannot answer this question.

It has taken me years to finally realize why I am here. I'm not alone in having faced a long journey to find my purpose in life and it still evolves. Sometimes it takes a while to figure out what we are meant to do or be in life. In my eyes, it is to serve other people and make their lives better in whatever way I can.

Of course, I am not always good at this and I forget. And I'm not alone in this, either. We all slip sometimes. It takes time and constant attention to change our mindset, but it is important to make the effort.

I believe everyone in life has, for the most part, good intentions. But most people, unless fully committed, will not put Give a Damn intentions into action. In constantly trying to do better, however, we make our own lives better. We serve ourselves by serving others. Isn't that what God wants us to do? The Give a Damn philosophy must take precedent over all of our actions. You know the truth now, so act upon it properly, as painful or difficult as it might be sometimes.

At the end of the day, you will feel terrific. There is nothing better in the world than helping someone in need, especially if it's someone who cannot help themselves.

When you give a damn, it has to become personal. One of the most important things we can do as individuals is to see others the same way that we see those we love. Think about it. Don't you give a damn for those you love? Why can't you do this on some level with others? We need to see other people as we see those we love—perhaps not to the same degree, but it needs to happen nonetheless.

We need to work toward treating people we don't know, including those from different economic, racial, and religious backgrounds, with respect and dignity.

The Bible says in Mark 12:31, "You shall love your neighbor as yourself," but it does not mean just your next-door neighbor. You need to think about how your actions might affect everyone, no matter who they are or where they are from. Most importantly, you must think about how far into the future these effects might reach.

For instance, that rusty nail left in the road could be driven over by someone and get lodged in their tire. Because this could potentially happen to anyone, you pick up the rusty nail and throw it away. We need to continually think this way and be aware of the effect that we have on our surroundings at all times.

I am a firm believer that, if you want something badly enough, you will go to great lengths, make the sacrifices, and put in the time to achieve it. And I am quite sure you can think of a circumstance in the past where you have had the energy and passion to obtain something that was vastly important to you. And you were successful!

If you feel you cannot do it on your own, ask God for help or enlist a loved one to support you in your efforts. Some people know how to give a damn because this type of attitude was adopted and nurtured from a young age—meaning their parents taught them well. It became instinctive because it was learned. These people just naturally think of others.

148

How can you learn to be a Give a Damn person? It's about awareness, attitude, practice, and a desire to make it happen. The famous radio host Earl Nightingale said, "We become what we think about." Look for ways to give a damn and you will find many opportunities.

Chapter 11 – Start a Revolution! How Do We Begin to Give a Damn?

One hundred years from now, it will not matter how much money you had, the house you lived in, or the kind of car you drove. I can give you all the guidelines, rules, and principles you need to give a damn, but these are just words. Until you use them to shape your actions, you can't call yourself a Give a Damn person.

It will take years for the Give a Damn revolution to really take shape and for people to shift into a Give a Damn focus and attitude. But the world may be different because you, as a Give a Damn person, were important in the life of all those you touched. Yet even these people will not be on this earth forever. But in the end, your maker (and mom) will know how many people you touched and how much you did to give a damn.

Giving a damn is a choice. It is the result of sincere intention, diligent effort, intelligent direction, and skillful execution. It also requires a humble manner of carrying yourself through the world.

Altruism can be learned and adopted. You may not feel that you have this inner quality now, but you can develop it by first laying a foundation of selfless behavior, one action and thought at a time. An altruistic act is not something you are obligated to do. It is something you do anyway, not for yourself but for others. Giving a damn represents a wise choice among many alternatives.

By reading this book to the end, I believe you are committed to being a Give a Damn person. No one is perfect. As I said before, we all can't be Nelson Mandela. Then again, we can certainly try our best to imitate him to some degree.

Now is the time to turn this awareness into action and start implementing a Give a Damn attitude into your everyday life. We need to think outside our own self-oriented personal domain as a way to give a damn.

Once you are more aware of your thoughts and their influence on your actions, you will begin to implement the process.

Once we do the right things often enough, they will become habitual to us on a daily—or even hourly—basis. You will then be able to behave in more generous and altruistic ways toward others.

Many people feel that they must put themselves and their work first in order to provide their families with food and shelter. However, you can easily serve others in so many different ways while you are still working to support yourself and your family. We can all give a damn even in small ways and live a more purposeful and giving life.

Write the phrase "Give a Damn" on index cards or sticky notes as a reminder and put them everywhere. Stick them on mirrors or doors so that you will see them every day. You might want to carry one around in your wallet or handbag to remind you of the philosophy; have one on your desk, in your car, or anywhere else that will provide you with a visible reminder to give a damn.

Better yet, buy the Give a Damn wristband, which can be your constant reminder wherever you go. Make sure you show your wristband to others, which shows your accountability.

Create your own herd mentality by forming a Give a Damn peer group. Leverage peer pressure to focus on your higher loves. Invite others to join you in giving a damn. This phrase will then become ingrained in your psyche and you will notice a gradual change in your attitude and your interactions with others.

The Give a Damn attitude is tied to a willingness to be responsible and make it happen. It starts with you. Just think if you saw someone else wearing the same Give a Damn wristband as you—and that there were millions of people doing the same thing. How would you feel? I would feel terrific, because perhaps I was making a difference in today's society or someone's life and others would be doing the same thing with me!

Learning to give a damn will not be easy. The best way to do it is to continually ask yourself this question, "How can I give a damn?" Each time you will get the right answer. You just have to listen. Don't try to justify behaviors in your mind when you know they are wrong. Pay attention and listen to the voice in your mind that is telling you the right thing to do, and don't ignore it.

Here are some simple things you can do to show that you give a damn in your personal life and in business:

- Volunteer for about 100 hours a year (that's less than two hours a week).

- Put the dishes in the dishwasher when you are finished. Then empty it completely when they're clean.

- Put away all mobile devices at dinnertime—or better yet, the whole evening.

- Scoop up your dog's waste, rather than leaving the mess for someone else.

- Keep your noise level down when others are sleeping or napping.

- Hurry across the street when a car stops for you.

- If you are in a grocery checkout lane and have a full cart, let someone who only has a few items go ahead of you.

- Say "thank you" whenever someone does something nice, "excuse me" when you impede someone's way, and "please" whenever you request something, whether verbal or written.

- Compliment or show appreciation all the time.

- Smile.

- Hold the door or elevator open for someone, regardless of gender and even if they are several steps away. Wait for them.

- Don't throw trash—even a single cigarette butt—out of your car window (you wouldn't throw it on the floor of your own residence, would you?).

- Pick up trash on the ground and throw it away.

- After using a shopping cart, put it in the corral reserved for carts or bring it back to the store entrance.

- If you hit or even bump an unoccupied car and it causes a dent or scratch of some kind, don't run off! Leave a note with your number on it.

- If a cashier gives you more in change than you should receive, give it back.

- Return a phone call, email, or text when someone you know has taken the time to reach out to you personally.

- Wave your hand as a gesture of thanks when someone lets you into traffic and let people merge into traffic without getting upset.

- When driving, use your turn signal and stay in the right-hand lane when not passing.

- Clean up the grass clippings when cutting grass, and don't blow them into the street for someone else to clean up.

- Take extra care to clean up after yourself in shared office spaces like restrooms or breakrooms.

- Think about spending other people's money—even corporate money—like it is your own.

- Stay late to help a colleague with a major project, even if it's not related to what you do.

- Have an open mind to everyone's ideas at your company, no matter what position they hold.

- As a team leader, recognize everybody when a project succeeds.

- Reward good behavior and use positive reinforcement for your team, but ditch the one-size-fits-all approach. Get to know your employees and what they value.

153

- Reward safe behaviors, rather than metrics that show a record of safety. This means that you can reward positive change as it's happening.

- Start team meetings with an expression of gratitude.

- As a customer service professional, admit when the company has made a mistake instead of making excuses.

- Keep a calm voice even with irate customers. Don't let their attitude control yours.

- Follow up with customers while working on a solution. Make sure they know you're not ignoring their problem.

- Write a thank you note to your favorite customer.

You and I could probably list hundreds more examples that show how to give a damn. Just take the initiative and do it. You will learn to give a damn by doing. Don't get discouraged if it takes longer than what you initially expect—you are not going to change your behavior overnight. Old habits die hard. But it is so important that you go for it with the confidence that you will succeed.

Whether it is an unexpected act of kindness, providing extraordinary customer service, or being sincerely interested in every word that a friend says, Give a Damn people usually have one thing in common: They consistently do more than what is expected of them and make doing more for others their primary focus.

I've heard it takes 21 days to learn a new habit or change one. For most people, it probably takes even longer. We have a choice, and we should choose to start each of those 21 or more days by saying, "I give a damn," and make this part of our daily routine.

What is really gratifying is this: When you do give a damn, you will begin to feel a great sense of satisfaction. As your old habits change and your new habits emerge, you'll be happier. You will be amazed at how good you will feel over the long term.

Don't be discouraged by those around you who don't give a damn. Sometimes people just don't care and we will never know the reason. Just trust how important this is for a better society with you leading the way. We need to do this one person and one incident at a time. Your actions will start to rub off on other people and they, too, will start to give a damn. It will take time, but all good things do. Commit and then just do it!

When do you feel your greatest happiness? It is in doing the simple things like sitting on the floor with your grandkids to play games, taking a walk to look at the stars, reading a child a story, or making a meal with your spouse. All of these activities are simple gifts from above.

Give a Damn needs to become your new way of thinking and doing over time. When you encounter a difficult situation or feel yourself slipping, repeat to yourself, "I give a damn," and you will get back on track.

Because you have persisted in reading this book, you now understand our challenges and hopefully agree with many of my assertions. You want to help change society for the better, one person at a time.

When I say to start a revolution, I mean it in a positive way. It's a movement in a positive direction and it starts with you! It won't be easy, but if you think about it, it won't be that hard either. After all, becoming more conscious and caring about other people is not something that requires any amount of money, physical strength, or talent.

It starts as a thought process that becomes ingrained in your brain every minute of every day, and then it just becomes your instinct. It is something everyone is capable of doing. We just need more and more people committed to this philosophy every day, one small deed and one thought at a time. And then together we can start a Give a Damn revolution.

It begins with passion and energy. With passion and energy, we can make just about anything happen. When we are passionate about something, we think about it all of the time and then it becomes part of our psyche.

It is what we want more than anything in the world, and we will go to great lengths to make it happen. You see this type of passion in athletes who are driven to succeed, in dedicated teachers, in prosperous entrepreneurs, and all other successful people regardless of their field.

When you give a damn, you create positive personal relationships with people. There is a ripple effect, and everyone wins. Other people will have a positive opinion of you and your organization, and they will strive to follow your example. Personal relationships are the fruit of the soul from which all successes begin and end. Give a Damn is your path to advancement and achievement, though it may not come in the ways you expect.

Let's go back to Tim Tebow as an example. His moral courage and integrity didn't bring him longevity in the NFL. But he continues to succeed as an author and speaker, and he makes a huge impact with his philanthropy. His foundation supports numerous efforts devoted to sick children, orphans, and people with special needs. And despite the critics' best efforts to undermine him, he is loving his minor league baseball career.

We can start a Give a Damn revolution through even the smallest acts of kindness. Each act will reverberate through society, eventually causing the overall thought process to change among people. Those who are the beneficiaries of good deeds usually go on to perform good deeds of their own.

People, especially those who are younger, tend to imitate what they see others do. If a Give a Damn attitude seeps into the culture at large, even the most resistant to this way of thinking will hopefully begin to change their ways to fit in with the rest of society! It's a process that will take time. But it's worth the effort.

One person at a time, and it begins with you. I think it is so important to change our beliefs and attitudes and learn to give a damn. It begins in the classroom, at home, in organizations, and in our own minds. It begins with knowing what is right and what is wrong and with everyone making the right choice.

We must start with our kids and stamp it into their psyche by teaching and modeling a Give a Damn attitude early on. The younger the kids are when they learn it, the easier it will be for them to implement it throughout their lives. But adults need it as well.

Changing a culture will take a long time but, if we want change, we must start now.

Individually you make a difference,

Collectively we change the world!

Good luck, and may God bless you always.

Acknowledgements

This book is dedicated to all my family and friends who encouraged me to write my first edition, especially my wife, Elizabeth Lewis; my Dad, C.S. Lewis; my twin sister, Kim Lewis James; my father-in-law, Doug Connell; Carl Gould; Christina Hildner; Aaron Edge; Sunay Patel; Tony Romanos; Thomas Brown; Mike Walker; A.J. Levin; and many more.

Special thanks to Amy Rose Pitonek who provided countless hours of editing and revisions for the first edition. Amy was the final impetus for completing it after many, many years of getting started.

And I cannot thank Molly Kramer and her team at Model Content enough for their help in taking Give a Damn to the next level. Molly has been an inspiration and driving force to vastly enhance this second edition. I could not have done it without her.

I want to thank the many people who supported me and the Louisiana Technology Council in recovering data off of the City of New Orleans' servers: Chris Reade and his team at Carrollton Technology Partners (now called Lookfar), Darryl d'Aquin and his team at CommTech Industries, Daryl Pfief and her team at Digital Forensic Solutions, and, of course, the FBI. Also, special thanks to the lawyers who assisted us with defending our actions during this whole incident.

Special thanks to Ali Hubbard Jones for her work in helping me with all aspects of my website and social media initiative. Ali has also been quite an inspiration in taking Give a Damn to the next level.

Special thanks to Steve Gleason and Paul Varisco for the support in providing the foreword to Give a Damn. Steve is truly a hero. Given all his struggles and his fight to find a cure for Lou

Gehrig's disease, he is the ultimate Give a Damn person.
Compared to everything Steve has been through, our Give a Damn
initiative should be really easy. Thank you, Steve, for all you do to
make people's lives better and giving us such a positive example to
follow.

I would also like to thank all the researchers cited in this
book. Special thanks go to Dr. Stephen G. Post, President of the
Institute for Research on Unlimited Love and Founding director of
the Center for Medical Humanities, Compassionate Care, and
Bioethics at the Stony Brook University School of Medicine.
Special thanks also go to Dr. Paul K. Piff, assistant professor of
psychological science at the University of California Irvine's
School of Social Ecology, where he leads the Morality, Emotion,
and Social Hierarchy Lab.

Finally, I would like to thank all the other people who
contributed their insights for this book. Special thanks goes to the
Delta Air Lines customer service and public relations teams,
especially Vice President of Customer Experience Integration
Charisse Evans.

Notes

The content in this book is a mixture of factual reporting and my own opinion. The reporting is based on many interviews, reports, and published studies.

I attempted to reach out to every individual and organization mentioned in the book to provide them with an opportunity to comment. I am extremely grateful to all the authors, researchers, and other sources whose expertise has made this book possible.

In some instances, identifying information was altered to protect patient privacy.

CHAPTER 1: – WHY I'M FED UP AND YOU SHOULD BE TOO!

[1]   E. Lane, "Inside the Ray Nagin investigation: A $50K bribe, a call from NJ and a mayor's downfall," The Times-Picayune, 19 May 2016.
[2]   C. DuBos, "Judge Ledet Pounds Nagin, Fields in WWL-TV Public Records Ruling," Gambit, 9 March 2009.
[3]   Louisiana Technology Council, "City of New Orleans E-mail Recovery Project Report," 2009.
[4]   Angel Arce-Torres obituary, The Hartford Courant, 14 May 2009.
[5]   R. Claiborne, B. Walker, and J. Brady, "Why Did No One Help Hit-and-Run Victim?" ABC News, 6 June 2008.
[6]   Beehphy, "Hero dog saves another after it was hit in the highway," 9 February 2009, retrieved from https://www.youtube.com/watch?v=-HJTG6RRN4E.

CHAPTER 2 – HOW DID WE GET HERE?

[7]   S.H. Konrath, E.H. O'Brien, and C. Hsing, "Changes in Dispositional Empathy in American College Students Over

Time: A Meta-Analysis," Personality and Social Psychology Review, vol. 15, no. 2, p. 180–198, 2011.

[8] Pew Research Center for The People & The Press, "How Young People View Their Lives, Futures and Politics: A Portrait of 'Generation Next,'" Washington, DC, 2007.

[9] G. Bishop, "In Tebow Debate, a Clash of Faith and Football," The New York Times, 7 November 2011.

[10] J. Branch and M. Pilon, "Tebow, a Careful Evangelical," The New York Times, 27 March 2012.

[11] N. Boyer, "An open letter to Colin Kaepernick, from a Green Beret-turned-long snapper," Army Times, 30 August 2016.

[12] S. Farmer, "The ex-Green Beret who inspired Colin Kaepernick to kneel instead of sit during the anthem would like to clear a few things up," Los Angeles Times, 17 September 2018.

[13] T. Collins, "Social media reacts as Kaepernick takes a knee in protest," CNET, 1 September 2016.

[14] S. Wyche, "Colin Kaepernick explains why he sat during national anthem," NFL.com, 27 August 2016.

[15] A. Roberts, "Group donates to Kenner city boosters in light of Nike ban," WVUE-Fox 8, 14 September 2018.

[16] D. Goldman, "Nike's Colin Kaepernick gamble is already paying off," CNN Money, 14 September 2018.

[17] "One Thing You will find in the Obits of Many Long Living People." Ohio State University, Laura Wallace, 13 June 13 2018.

[18] IBM, "Chronological History of IBM: 1980s," retrieved from https://www-03.ibm.com/ibm/history/history/decade_1980.html on 6 August 2018.

[19] American Academy of Pediatrics Council on Communications and Media, "Media and Young Minds," Pediatrics, vol. 138, no. 5, p. 1-6, 2016.

[20] The Nielsen Company, "The Nielsen Total Audience Report: Q1 2018," 2018.

CHAPTER 3 – GIVING A DAMN STARTS AT HOME

[21] D. Brooks, The Road to Character, New York, NY: Random House, 2015.

[22] Holy Bible, New International Version®, 1973, 1978, 1984, 2011 by Biblica, Inc.®

CHAPTER 4 – GIVE A DARN AT SCHOOL

[23] S. Grace, "Stelly Plan marked golden era of tax reform," The Advocate, 2 June 2018.

[24] The Task Force on Structural Changes in Budget and Tax Policy, "Louisiana's Opportunity: Comprehensive Solutions for a Sustainable Tax and Spending Structure," 2017.

[25] J. O'Donoghue, "Louisiana's budget is a hot mess: How we got here," The Times-Picayune, 12 February 2016.

[26] Organisation for Economic Co-operation and Development, "OECD Better Life Index," retrieved from http://www.oecdbetterlifeindex.org/topics/education/ on 15 August 2018.

[27] E. Hanushek and L. Wößmann, "Education Quality and Economic Growth," The International Bank for Reconstruction and Development / The World Bank, Washington, DC, 2007.

[28] National Center for Education Statistics, "The Condition of Education: Educational Attainment of Young Adults," retrieved from https://nces.ed.gov/programs/coe/indicator_caa.asp on 15 August 2018.

[29] C. Belfield, B. Bowden, A. Klapp, H. Levin, R. Shand, and S. Zander, "The Economic Value of Social and Emotional Learning," Center for Benefit-Cost Studies in Education, Teachers College, Columbia University, New York, NY, 2015 (revised).

[30]   R. Pausch, "Carnegie Mellon University: Randy Pausch's Web Site," retrieved from https://www.cs.cmu.edu/~pausch/ on 15 August 2018.

[31]   Carnegie Mellon University, "Randy's Story," retrieved from https://www.cmu.edu/randyslecture/story/index.html on 15 August 2018.

CHAPTER 5 – GIVE A DAMN ON TEAMS

[32]   B. Martel, "Brees: Focus on keeping Saints together," The San Diego Union-Tribune, 20 January 2012.

[33]   NFL.com Wire Reports, "Drew Brees signs $100 million contract with New Orleans Saints," NFL.com, 15 July 2012.

[34]   D.O. Ledbetter, "Payton regrets making choke gesture to Freeman," Atlanta Journal-Constitution, 20 December 2017.

[35]   W. Covil and A. Bryan, "Locals flabbergasted after VDOT simply paints over dead raccoon in road." WTVR-CBS 6, 15 July 2016.

[36]   G. Russell, "Nagin aides rack up charges on city credit card," The Times-Picayune, 14 May 2008.

[37]   A.L. Rubenstein, M.B. Eberly, T.W. Lee, and T.R. Mitchell, "Surveying the forest: A meta-analysis, moderator investigation, and future-oriented discussion of the antecedents of voluntary employee turnover," Personnel Psychology, vol. 71, no. 1, p. 23–65, 2018.

[38]   K. Spain, "New Orleans Saints release Deuce McAllister," The Times-Picayune, 17 February 2009.

[39]   Associated Press, "Saints release injury-riddled RB McAllister to cut costs," NFL.com, 17 February 2009.

[40]   M. Scott, "Deuce McAllister joins WVUE-Fox 8 as New Orleans Saints analyst," The Times-Picayune, 19 July 2018.

CHAPTER 6 – GIVE A DAMN IN MANAGEMENT

[42]   S. Roberts, "Delivering Culture Change," Training Journal, p. 20-23, April 2018.

[42]   R. Jana, "My Company Grew 800 Percent in a Year After I Made This Mindset Shift Grow," Entrepreneur, 3 May 2018.

[43]   Technology Employment Ranking, TechAmerica – CyberStates, October 2011.

[44]   D. Jones and M. Ballé, "Lean is a people-centric system," ISE Magazine, vol. 48, no. 10, p. 26-30, 2016.

CHAPTER 7 – GIVE A DAMN IN CUSTOMER SERVICE

[45]   The Stevie Awards for Sales & Customer Service, "Delta Air Lines – Katie Suitter," retrieved from https://stevieawards.com/sales/delta-air-lines-katie-suitter on 17 September 2018.

CHAPTER 8 – GIVE A DAMN IN YOUR COMMUNITY

[46]   "Princess Diana's 15 most powerful and inspirational quotes," The Telegraph, 29 June 2018.

[47]   S.G. Post, "Rx It's Good to be Good (G2BG) 2017 Commentary: Prescribing Volunteerism for Health, Happiness, Resilience, and Longevity," American Journal of Health Promotion, vol. 31, no. 2, p. 163-172, 2017.

[48]   Associated Press, "Driver who tossed kittens out of window on Causeway sought," The Times-Picayune, 30 September 2009.

[49]   R. Atkinson and T. Rodgers, "Pleasure Zones and Murder Boxes: Online Pornography and Violent Video Games as Cultural Zones of Exception," The British Journal of Criminology, vol. 56, no. 6, p. 1291–1307, 2016.

[50]   U.S. Department of Justice, Federal Bureau of Investigation, "A Study of Active Shooter Incidents in the

United States Between 2000 and 2013," Washington, DC, 2014.

[51] Department of Homeland Security, United States Secret Service, National Threat Assessment Center, "Mass Attacks in Public Spaces - 2017," Washington, DC, 2018.

[52] S. Towers, A. Gomez-Lievano, M. Khan, A. Mubayi, and C. Castillo-Chavez, "Contagion in Mass Killings and School Shootings," PLOS One, vol. 10, no. 7, pp. 1-12, 2015.

[53] M. Pearce, "Adam Lanza's files show him as another shooter caught up in Columbine," Los Angeles Times, 27 November 2013.

[54] S.D. James, "Psychology of Virginia Tech, Columbine Killers Still Baffles Experts," ABC News, 16 April 2009.

[55] C. Mckinley, "Key Findings From James Holmes Evaluation Interviews," WPVI-ABC 6, 5 June 2015.

[56] A. Hairan, "A Profile of the Taliban's Propaganda Tactics," HuffPost, 3 April 2010.

CHAPTER 9 – GIVE A DAMN IN GOVERNMENT

[57] "Profile: Nelson Mandela's long walk," CNN, 26 June 2008.

[58] M. Gilens and B.I. Page, "Testing Theories of American Politics: Elites, Interest Groups, and Average Citizens," Perspectives on Politics, vol. 12, no. 3, p. 564-581, 2014.

[59] SCOTUSblog, "Citizens United v. Federal Election Commission," retrieved from http://www.scotusblog.com/case-files/cases/citizens-united-v-federal-election-commission/ on 17 September 2018.

[60] Center for Responsive Politics, "OpenSecrets.org: 2018 Campaign Contribution Limits," retrieved from https://www.opensecrets.org/overview/limits.php on 17 September 2018.

[61] Pew Research Center, "The Public, the Political System and the American Democracy: Most say 'design and

structure' of government need big changes," Washington,
DC, 2018.

[62]   National Archives, "Documents Related to Brown v. Board
of Education," retrieved from
https://www.archives.gov/education/lessons/brown-v-board
on 15 August 2018.

[63]   S. Greytak, A. Bannon, A. Falce, and L. Casey,
"Bankrolling the Bench: The New Politics of Judicial
Elections 2013-2014," Justice at Stake, Brennan Center for
Justice, and National Institute on Money in State Politics,
Washington, DC, 2015.

[64]   H. Ibsen, An Enemy of the People, New York, NY:
Penguin Random House, 1977.

[65]   F. Donze, "Nagin administration dumps e-mail search
experts," The Times-Picayune, 16 July 2009.

[66]   "Ray Nagin sentenced to 10 years in prison for public
corruption," The Times-Picayune, 9 July 2014.

CHAPTER 10 – CHANGING FROM THE INSIDE

[67]   C.R. Swindoll, "Insight for Living Ministries: Attitudes
Color Quote Print," retrieved from
https://store.insight.org/p-1389-attitudes-quote-color-
print.aspx on 10 August 2018.

CHAPTER 11 – START A REVOLUTION! HOW DO WE BEGIN TO GIVE
A DAMN?

[68]   B. Sims Jr., "Using Positive-Reinforcement Programs to
Effect Culture Change," Employment Relations Today, vol.
41, no. 2, p. 43-47, 2014.